THE
FINANCIAL SECTOR
OF THE AMERICAN
ECONOMY

edited by

STUART BRUCHEY
UNIVERSITY OF MAINE

A GARLAND SERIES

BANKING IN AN UNREGULATED ENVIRONMENT

California, 1878–1905

LYNNE PIERSON DOTI

GARLAND PUBLISHING, Inc.
NEW YORK & LONDON / 1995

Library of Congress Cataloging-in-Publication Data

Pierson Doti, Lynne.
    Banking in an unregulated environment : California, 1878–
1905 / Lynne Pierson Doti.
        p.   cm. — (The financial sector of the American econ-
omy)
    Includes bibliographical references and index.
    ISBN 0-8153-1873-1 (alk. paper)
    1. Banks and banking—California—History.   2. Banks and
banking—Deregulation—California—History.   I. Title.
II. Series.
HG2611.C2D67   1995
332.1'09794—dc20   95-14436
                                                                            CIP

Printed on acid-free, 250-year-life paper
Manufactured in the United States of America

To Jim

CONTENTS

TABLES

PREFACE

The study of financial history has become increasingly important in the last five to ten years. The 1987 crash of the stock market brought renewed attention to theories about the relationship of financial markets to the rest of the economy. Alan Greenspan, other Federal Reserve policy makers and Congress, impatient to cure inflation and recession, have become bold about testing theories on the real world. The Soviet Union collapsed, leaving a multitude of countries without any useable financial structure at all. If financial history has evidence to present on how things work, the world is ready to listen.

While this work is based on my 1978 dissertation, there have been numerous revisions. First, the narrative has been updated to include the insights from my subsequent research for *Banking in the American West* and for *California Bankers 1848 to 1993.*[1] Second, the original work benefitted little from the miracles of the computer age, so, without changing the basic tests, many calculations have been reworked to use the more sophisticated techniques and greater accuracy modern computers make so easily available. Third, naturally, I have taken the opportunity to correct as many errors as possible.

I would again like to thank my dissertation committee who guided the original work and sparked an interest in a subject that has now occupied me for almost 20 years: Roger Ransom, James Earley and Maureen Cropper. In addition I wish to express my gratitude for the support and encouragement provided by Professors Donald Booth, Jim Doti, Homa Shabahang, and other colleagues at Chapman University. My student assistant for this revision was a highly capable undergraduate, Richard Runyon. Student Celine Douchez, from Chapman's MBA program, assisted with clerical duties.

I would also like to thank my husband and my children: Adam, whose early childhood was marked by my first struggles with this work, and Cara, who suffered through the second version; for their patience and forbearance.

Lynne Pierson Doti
Orange, California

1. Lynne Pierson Doti and Larry Schweikart, *Banking in the American West: From Gold Rush to Deregulation* (Norman,OK: University of Oklahoma Press, 1991); Pierson Doti and Schweikart, *California Bankers 1848 - 1993* (Needham Heights, MA: Ginn Press, 1994).

I

INTRODUCTION

The work of financial historians is to search out information on financial institutions and markets from the past and to test current theories with this data. The study of financial history has provided data for testing theories mostly in two fields of economics: financial structure and performance, and economic development. Theories of bank performance and structure have been tested using historical data. In this area, historical data has several advantages over contemporary data. Capital markets were more segregated and, because banks and their close substitutes were subject to less regulation and entry restrictions, they were freer to respond to market forces. This produced a variety of situations for analysis and comparison. The study of economic development has also benefitted from availability of historical data. Economists are still searching for explanations of the development process, but current theories allocate a fairly important influence to financial factors. Most of these theories of economic growth are based on the growth patterns of already developed countries.

Both areas of study are in urgent need of information. Bank failures continue to be a problem in the United States and other countries, and the recent failure of the international BCCI proved that the increasing size and ease of international transactions may bring even larger problems in banking. The proper structure of banking and money creation and role of financial institutions in development has just become an area of interest to the many new countries created by the demise of the Soviet Union, as well as to the countries plagued by continuing poverty.

MONEY, CREDIT AND THE ECONOMY

Perhaps the most familiar case of using historical financial data to test a contemporary theory is *A Monetary History of the United States* by Milton Friedman and Anna Schwartz.[1] Although offered as a narrative to accompany statistical series of money supply data, it continually relates the statistical results to the monetary theory presented in other works by Friedman.[2] Philip Cagan also used historical material to test the quantity theory in "The Monetary

Dynamics of Hyperinflation" and other essays.[3] The entire volume of *Studies in the Quantity Theory of Money* is devoted to the same type of work,[4] and the Federal Reserve Bank of St. Louis is continually engaged in research using more recent historical data.[5] Peter Temin uses previously collected historical material to test Keynesian and quantity theories about the causes of the depression of the 1930s.[6]

Money supply creation is not the only role attributed to banks in the economy. The act of granting credit has been ascribed with the power to create prosperity and depression. While Alan Greenspan reputedly discovered this only in 1994, earlier economists often tested credit volume, distinct from money creation, in business cycle theory. Alvin Hansen contends, for instance, that business cycles have been a phenomena that depend on money and credit generation.[7] Wesley Mitchell portrays financial intermediaries as passive participants in business cycles, who obligingly expand credit at businessmen's request during prosperous times.[8] Ludwig von Mises felt financial intermediaries could lengthen a business cycle. In an older tradition, he also felt economic expansion inevitably led to collapse. But the expansion of credit could postpone the collapse.[9] R.G. Hawtrey viewed the changes in the level of trade as reflections of the changes in the monetary sector of the economy.[10]

Post-Keynesian economists also stressed the role of financial intermediaries in business fluctuations. John Maynard Keynes and his contrasting contemporary, Irving Fisher, both concerned themselves with the role of credit. Fisher had a rather traditional American distrust of financial operations. This distrust is clearly expressed in *The Theory of Interest*, where borrowers are sadly lacking in self control.[11] In *Booms and Depressions*, he explains how "excessive" debt causes depressions.[12] The very existence of a banking system is a threat to the economy because it facilitates debt.

John Maynard Keynes saw the role of the banking system as a stabilizing economic force in *A Treatise on Money*.[13] Bankers, by adjusting interest rates assure savings will equal investment. This classical view is altered in *The General Theory*.[14]Additional bank credit, he says, cannot allow increased investment without increased savings. However, he states "if the grant of a bank credit to an entrepreneur additional to the credits already existing allows him to make an addition to current investment which would not have occurred otherwise, income will necessarily be increased ...."[15] So an increase in bank credit might have far reaching effects on the economy.

Modern theorists have all noted the importance of the banking system in the economy. Although James Duesenberry contends that tightened credit cannot alone cause a depression, his theories of cycles give bankers a primary role.[16]

In the past three decades, much attention has been directed to the behavior of financial intermediaries and their ability to thwart government monetary policy. Recent works still struggle with the question of whether banks passively react to business cycles, or cause them. Most writers however have accepted the fact that the latter is at least a possibility and direct their attention to a technique for controlling bankers' behavior. Milton Friedman and his followers have focussed on the control of the money supply, but others feel this would imperfectly control bankers.[17] A 1972 study by Philip Cagan was an early attempt to differentiate between the impact of money supply and credit changes on the economy.[18]

MONETARY SYSTEMS

With the generally acknowledged importance of money and credit to the economy, regulation was inevitable. Governments, at all levels sought control. Since banks are the conduit to the economy for both money and credit, the banking system became a regulated industry. While probably inevitable, whether this is desirable is an area of controversy. The first modern history of U.S. banking history, Bray Hammond's *Banks and Politics in America from the Revolution to the Civil War* answered this question in 1957 with a resounding "yes."[19] Even free market advocate Milton Friedman has admitted that money creation and distribution is an industry that requires regulation.

More recently, some economists have developed the theory that banks produce a steadier flow of money and credit without any regulation at all. Examples from this group include George A. Selgin, *The Theory of Free Banking*, David Glasner, *Free Banking and Monetary Reform*, and Lawrence White, *Free Banking in Britain: Theory, Experience and Debate, 1800-1845.*[20] *Free Banking: Theory, History, and a Laissez-Faire Model* by Larry J. Sechrest suggests that free banking, in the sense of allowing banks to be governed only by the market forces, combined with a system of fractional gold reserves provides a system which will satisfy the need for a credit and monetary policy. He suggests that such a system will prevent money from being the cause of economic disturbances, provide a stable economic environment, and offset major disturbances that arise from nonmonetary sources, goals suggested earlier by Milton Friedman.[21]

FINANCIAL THEORIES OF BANKING

To test any of these theories we need accurate data. To learn how bank behavior affects the economy, economists should seek to determine how banks were behaving with different structures during periods of expansion and recession. History provides these examples, but historical data needs improvement in accessibility and accuracy.

Once economists understand the relationship between banking actions and economic change, they would naturally turn to the examination of the causes underlying those bank actions, wishing to discover techniques to provoke the desired reaction. Many of the current theories of bank behavior stem from the portfolio theories of Markowitz, Sharpe and others. In these theories bankers arrange their assets to maximize return while avoiding risk.[22] In modern times bankers behavior has been severely modified by government regulation. To properly determine the impact of regulation it is necessary to test a variety of levels of regulation. Historical data could provide researchers with a set of banks less regulated than present day counterparts.[23]

Researchers studying the impact of bank size, concentration, and branching would also benefit from more easily accessible historical material.[24] As debate currently wages about a bill to allow nationwide branching, the current work on branching has not yielded a decisive conclusion about its impact on concentration and service. The fact that few states allowed unrestricted branching until this past decade makes it difficult to test its effects. The discoveries of economies of scale may occur because of the recent requirements of large reserves, and other regulations, or in spite of them. The small variation in reserve requirements makes a test of these theories difficult, and even before the 1980 Deregulation and Monetary Control Act, most states have similar bank reserve requirements. The availability of more historical data could improve knowledge about the impact of branching and reserve requirements.

Theories of economic development have vital interest to a major portion of the world. Most of the current theories have been based on the experience of already-industrialized nations. Almost every comprehensive theory notes the importance of financial systems in the development process. Joseph Schumpeter's theory is one early example. He portrays economies as tending to a steady state with no unemployed resources, but no increases in production. Growth occurs with the arrival of an entrepreneur, an individual with an innovation--combining the resources in new ways. This individual's superior ideas allow excess profit, and the scramble to imitate constitutes the expansionary force in the economy. The full employment of resources at the start of the growth means that the innovator cannot try his ideas with previously idle resources. All income from production is committed to maintaining the circular flow. The creation of purchasing power for the entrepreneur is in the expansion of credit. "Credit detaches productive means (already employed somewhere) from the circular flow and allots them to new combinations." Although the process detaches goods from their old employments and puts them in new uses, "it cannot be described entirely in term of goods, something essential occurs in the sphere of money and credit."[25]

Virtually every modern study of development has researched the role of financial institutions. Alexander Gerschenkron and Rondo Cameron wrestle with the problem of whether the development of financial intermediaries is growth inducing or growth induced. Gerschenkron suggests institutional development which increased capital mobility played an important role in European development and Cameron tentatively concludes that the American banking system was a passive reaction to growth.[26] In his study of financial structures and development, Raymond Goldsmith states, "One of the most important problems in the field of finance, if not the most important one, almost everyone would agree, is the effect that financial structure and development have on economic growth."[27] He uses the available historical material to develop generalizations or regularities apparent in the process of development. He found, for instance, that the ratio of financial assets to wealth rises during development, then levels off. More developed countries have higher ratios than less developed countries.[28] He complains his work is limited by inadequate data: "To assess the role of financial development and structure in economic growth we may turn...to economic theory or to economic history...with the present lack of sufficiently intensive historical studies of financial development we cannot get definite answers."[29] After almost 25 years, this problem still exists.

Douglas North centers his development theories around change in institutional arrangements and also presents the history of developed countries as support for these ideas. He contends that capital was able to move easily enough in the United States' industrialization period to avoid hampering development.[30]

These and other prominent economists in the fields of economic development recognize that financial structure may reflect or may cause changes in the economy. To define the role of finance, more accurate and complete information about history must be obtained. Among developed nations, the United States perhaps is unique in the fact that little central control of banking was exerted during the industrialization process. Therefore the behavior of the financial sector of the United States during its period of industrialization is of concern to students of economic development.

Theories concerning banker's behavior, economic performance and development all have been based primarily upon data from the history of European countries and the United States. Yet the history of finance in this country is rather limited. Much of the historical work in this field is regarded as impressionistic rather than scientific by many economists. Basically narrative histories of note include those by John J. Knox, Fritz Redlich and Paul Trescott. Although comprehensive, these works cannot be termed definitive. The Knox book is primarily the result of a series of his papers on banking. Knox died before completing the collection of material for his intended book "worthy of the title 'History of Banking in the United States,'"[31] An associate of Knox at the Comptroller's office, William Greene, cooperated with *Banker's Magazine* to achieve the works Knox planned. The book is a particularly interesting source for the years when Knox served as Comptroller of the Currency, 1872-1884. It also has a section written by several authors, detailing banking history in each of the United States. It also has a chapter on state banking. The result, though disjointed, has a great deal of valuable information.

The Trescott book is more entertaining, but contains much less original material.[32] Biographical narrative dominates, and only commercial banks are discussed. The book would be useful as an introduction to the most important bank history, Redlich's *The Molding of American Banking*. Redlich devotes most of the book to biography and clearly states his Schumpterian belief that men are the carriers of economic development.[33] He also provides descriptions of the political debate and circumstances surrounding the enactment of some important pieces of bank legislation (for example, the Louisiana Banking Act of 1842).

These three major works are supplemented by Bray Hammond's exhaustive history of *antebellum* banking. The four books, and many earlier works,[34] share a common bias which Richard Sylla has called the "soundness tradition."[35] The viewpoint judges financial institutions by the standard of short-term, self-liquidating lending, adequate specie reserves, and metallic money. Redlich, for instance, compliments a nineteenth century banker who "rightly saw the flaw in contemporary reasoning, that by substituting paper money for coin, the national economy gained additional capital to be used for productive purposes."[36] Similar examples can be cited from the other works. Instead of seeking to explore banks' role in society, these writers have predefined the role and use history mainly as an example of the necessity for government control of the financial industry.

This belief has been questioned by some writers of a more contemporary school of economics. One of the issues first approached by the cliometrics devotees was the necessity for regulating banks. As many of the traditional works dealt with the *antebellum* period, newer works also sought to explore a period when there were sharp contrasts in the degrees of control of banks. J. Van Fenstermaker supplied numerical data on federalist years, and Peter Temin and Hugh Rockoff produced new studies of the demise of the second bank of the U.S., and the free banking era.[37] Peter Temin showed that the conflict between Nicholas Biddle and Andrew Jackson probably had very little to do with the inflation of the early 1830's, or with the subsequent depression. This contrasts sharply with previous work, which generally blamed the economic problems of the decade on Biddle, Jackson, or greedy bankers. Stanley Engerman supported these conclusions by making use of the counterfactual hypothesis technique. He simulated a world with the Second Bank still in existence in the 1850's and compared this with actual national income.[38] Hugh Rockoff regressed money holdings per capita on wealth, urbanization, and a dummy variable representing the level of bank regulation in a state to find that the level of control of banking did not have any significant impact on public confidence in their banks.[39] The conclusion was amplified in a later article which shows banks recognized that overissue would depreciate their currency, causing them to limit themselves to a relatively safe position.[40] Rockoff's work generally supported Redlich's observation on the free banking period after 1840, that as specie reserves were voluntary in most states, banks could operate two ways: they could keep little in reserve because it was unproductive capital, or they could keep high specie reserves to establish a reputation for safety. This reputation would have compensated for interest foregone by attracting high deposits and larger circulation of notes.[41]

Lance Davis was the first of the quantitatively oriented economic historians to focus on U.S. history in the later part of the nineteenth century.[42] His 1965 article on the investment market remains a standard against which subsequent works are measured. Pointing out that capital must not only be accumulated, but must be mobilized, Davis explored the evidence of capital movement in the United States from 1870 to 1914. He noted that, in this country, capital had to move from old to new industries and also from one geographic area to another. The savings accrued in the Northeast, and the demand for capital occurred in the South and West. Davis used the Comptroller of the Currency reports on the national banks for data to test for differences between regions in a proxy for interest rates. The proxy consisted of gross or net earnings divided by earnings assets. Gross earnings were available from 1888 to 1914; net earnings were used for earlier years. Using unweighted averages of these ratios for banks in each of five regions of the country, Davis found significant differences. These differentials showed a marked decrease sometime in the late 1890's, although the decline does not occur with respect to the Pacific region.[43] Davis' results suggest that there was a gradual movement toward a national short term capital market. Further, rates in the Eastern regions narrowed before those in the West and South. Differences between reserve city banks declined before of non-reserve city banks.

Davis then examined various sources of interregional mobility of capital. He first contested an early study by R.M. Breckenridge, that claimed to have discovered permanent interregional interest rate differences due to the prohibition of national branch banking.[44] Davis contended that declining differentials during the period do not support the Breckenridge hypothesis. There were, according to Davis, three factors working to decrease interest differentials. First, there was direct solicitation of funds by banks in areas with high interest rates. The Comptroller of the Currency remarked upon these flows of funds with disfavor in his 1890 report.[45] The second possible source of capital mobility was the practice of individual banks rediscounting paper.

Breckenridge provided figures on the proportion of rediscounted loans to all loans and discounts. This proportion ranged up to eight percent, but the average was only about 1 1/2 percent. It appeared that banks in high interest rate areas discounted more frequently than banks in areas with low interest rates, but Davis doubted that the volume of these transactions was sufficient to significantly improve capital mobility. The most important source of mobile funds was probably the evolution of a market for commercial paper, as the appearance of the market coincided with the initial movement toward national convergence of earning to asset ratios.

Davis also attempted to illustrate declining differences in long term interest rates. He had little data on these rates, as most of the national banks' assets were short term, but a survey by the U.S. Bureau of the Census summarized mortgage interest rates for 1880 to 1889. These figures showed declining differences between regions.[46] For years outside the 1880 to 1889 period, little evidence was available. There are several reports researching individual counties or towns, but these do not allow interregional comparison.[47] Davis felt there was some indication of generally declining mortgage rate differentials in this material. To test this observation, Davis used balance sheets of savings banks taken from the Comptroller's reports to develop a proxy for long term interest rates. Reasoning that a bank in a high-interest area would place a larger portion of its assets into loans than would a banker in low-interest area, Davis used loans divided by the sum of loans plus securities for an interest rate proxy. Minimal data and heroic assumptions cloud the results, but Davis felt there was support for the hypothesis that interest rate differentials decreased. The time period 1870 to 1885 shows more evidence of declining differential than the period 1885 to 1914.[48]

Overall, Davis' conclusions were that interest rates differed between regions in the period 1870 to 1914. These interest rate differences reflected immobility of capital. The development of a commercial paper market late in the century helped overcome this immobility, as did several other institutional changes. Interest rate differentials declined over the period, although this decline may not have occurred for long-term rates during the period 1885 to 1905. The South and the Far West still show evidence of isolation from the national financial markets even by 1914.[49]

A short time later, Richard Sylla's investigations revealed the national banking system's impact on banking during the 1863 to 1913 era.[50] Sylla felt the effect of government's intervention in banking was to restrain the growth of the banking system, which created local monopolies in rural areas, and to provide a link between banks which allowed for the transfer of funds from agricultural areas to industrial areas.[51] Sylla showed that the national banking system tended to restrict banking. His support was first, in major agricultural areas of the country, the average capital and the capital to deposit ratios of the banks were below the minimum required for national banks, even by 1900. Second, national banks were infrequently located in rural areas because of the prohibition of their lending on real estate. While these factors would seem to have affected only the tendency of banks to be chartered by the federal, rather than the state government, Sylla contended the rules affected all bank information. The state chartered banks had low capital requirements, fewer loan restrictions, and less control over their activities than national banks. In spite of these advantages, their assets were small compared to those of national banks. The tax levied on state bank notes affected bankers in agricultural areas most, because the customers in these areas were resistant to accepting substitutes for notes. Because of these factors, Sylla hypothesized that country bankers had monopolies over the local lending, and urban bankers operated in a setting of competition.

Under the national banking system, reserves were required of all member banks. For all but New York banks, part of these reserves could be held as deposits in other banks. These reserve accounts normally were interest-bearing. Therefore the rural banker could invest funds in city banks in preference to increased lending to the local market. This kept rural interest rates on the average higher than city rates and encouraged capital to flow from areas where it was scarce to areas where low interest rates indicated abundant capital.

Sylla used the ratio of net earnings to earnings assets to test for monopoly power. As the rates of net earnings differed, with rural banks earning higher returns, the theory that differences in interest rates were caused by difference in cost was not supported, and his conclusion was that country banks could have had greater monopoly power than banks in more urban areas. Sylla also tested for variance in the quantity of loans produced by city and rural banks. The presumably monopolistic rural banks should have made fewer loans than a similar urban bank. Comparison of loan to asset ratios illustrated this difference. In tests of Comptroller data from 1870, 1875, 1880, 1885, 1890, 1900 and 1910, Sylla found the loan to asset ratio generally higher in cities than in the county areas. The difference declined over the period.

Noting that these differences in ratios may be attributable to higher deposit to equity ratios in the cities, Sylla tested profit rates. Using net earnings divided by capital plus surplus for each national bank, he found profits higher for country banks than for city banks, which indicated the possibility of more monopoly power in the rural areas. Sylla also studied the amount of reserves on deposits. Using Margaret Myers' report on New York banks, he found country bankers had excess reserves on deposits throughout the period 1875-1914.[52] Sylla also found the balance due to country banks, net of amount due from country banks, averaged between six and ten percent of country bank assets. The figures peak in 1900 and thereafter decline.

Sylla concluded that rural bankers were probably price discriminating monopolists whose ability to transfer funds to urban areas assisted in the urbanization of the United States in the late nineteenth century.

The Sylla and Davis results have been directly contested . By using the same national banking data, Gene Smiley arrived at different conclusions about late nineteenth century banking.[53] His basic technique was to take gross earnings as a ratio of earnings assets, but the calculation technique differs from that of Davis. Earning assets were divided into three groups: private earning assets, U.S. bonds, and reserve deposits. An attempt was made to divide the gross earnings into that which was attributable to each category of assets, using a residual technique. Smiley then approximated ratios of earnings to private earnings assets for each state and reserve city separately. The majority of these private earnings assets were loans, although stocks, securities and local and corporate bonds were included. He contended this ratio is a good approximation of interest rates, and illustrated this by comparing the ratios with estimates published by the Comptroller of the Currency in 1902. Smiley then grouped these figures by regions, which differ slightly from those of the Comptroller reports.[54] An analysis of the dispersion of the gross rates of return by state showed no pronounced trend of rate convergence. The rates for non-reserve city banks diverge through the eighteen-nineties, then slowly converge after that. By 1913, the dispersion had declined to its 1890 level. Smiley attributed this behavior to the differential impact of the 1907 depression. Reserve cities, however, showed some increased divergence between 1888 and 1913 when all reserve cities were used, but showed the same trends as non-reserve cities when no new reserve cities were added after 1891. The lowest rates of difference appeared after 1907, leading Smiley to conclude that some rapid change occurred which led to more capital mobility between cities. Smiley agreed with Davis in attributing the change to the development of commercial paper, although he contends the development was rapid rather than gradual.[55]

John James was the next researcher to pursue these issues. In a series of 1976 articles, he sought to test the influences of the commercial paper market and the 1900 changes in national banking law on monopoly power.[56] First, he tried to test for the ability of concentration to explain variations between regional interest rates. James developed a test of the impact of market power on interest rates.[57] The model he developed integrated many concepts of basic portfolio theory as expressed by Sharpe and others.[58] However, many of the factors in the model are not observable and his model must be modified for testing.[59] The average rate of return on commercial loans was calculated by a complex residual technique. From gross earnings, James subtracted his calculations of the gross return to earning assets other than commercial loans. He took the nominal interest on the par value for the return on all government bonds. Returns from the deposits at other banks were estimated at two percent.[60] James accepted Macaulay's 1938 estimates of the return on railroad bonds, and made them the rate of return for all other bonds and stocks held by the banks. After these calculated amounts were subtracted from gross earnings, the remainder was considered the return to loans and discounts.[61] The risk factors were indicated by previous and present losses. The Comptroller's report provided the combined total of losses and premiums by area. Losses and premiums were reported separately in three annual reports and James assumed that the proportions established in these years indicate the division appropriate for all years.

The monopoly power variable is the most important variable in the study, and probably the most inaccurate. Monopoly power, as measured by James, is simply the number of banks per capita by state. Population figures used in his study were interpolated from census figures, therefore not only smooth any differences in monopoly power over a state, but the procedure based all the regression data on only two census years. The source for the number of banks is also flawed. The accuracy of data in *All Bank Statistics* is open to question. There is also no source for many of the bank statistics for years before 1896;

James used extrapolated numbers for earlier years. Although a technique was used to reduce statistical problems involved in such a large regression, these problems further reduce confidence in the results.[62]

James found that for most states the market power coefficients were significant and negative. Interest rates were lower where monopoly power was less. Only about one quarter of the Western states conformed to these results. The South and Midwest fit most uniformly. James felt the West consisted of extremely segmented markets, so that changes in bank density would have had little overall effect on interest rates. In large reserve cities, where it is expected that competition would have been greatest, the monopoly power coefficient was positive.[63]

In another article, James assumed the existence of monopoly where he tested for the effect of the commercial paper market and the changes in the national banking laws on concentration. His technique in this article are also interesting.[64] The explanations of declining interest rate differentials given by Davis and Sylla were directly compared, using the same model as in the article discussed above. James showed that changes in estimated risk variables were not sufficient to explain the declines in the interest rate differentials. Therefore, he contended barriers to capital mobility must have existed. These may have been broken down by the advance of the commercial paper market into new areas. James contended banks always had access to the commercial paper market through their correspondent relationships. However, the opening of a commercial paper market could have lowered interest rates by allowing local banks to diversify their portfolios and decrease risk. It also could have lowered rates by giving borrowers a source of financing other than the local bank. His loss rate coefficient was tested for its responsiveness to the introduction of the commercial paper dealer in six areas. The results were inconclusive. The market power variable did not shift in response to the introduction of commercial paper sales in four other areas. His other tests also failed to support the expansion of the commercial paper market as the explanation of declining monopoly.

James also contended Sylla's explanation of declining interest rate differentials was inaccurate. Sylla's explanation of the decline centered on the 1900 changes in the National Banking Act. While it is true that the number of national banks increased more rapidly after 1900, the number of state banks increased over the entire period. Also, many of the new national banks were merely conversions of state banks.

Running a cross-sectional by state, James found interest rates highly correlated with the states' minimum capital requirement for 1909. James also regressed the changes in interest rates in 1888-1911 by state on the 1909 minimum capital requirements and found that states with lower capital requirements experienced more decreases in interest rates. Although these tests did not reflect the many changes in capital requirements (most changes were increases) that occurred over the period, they do point out the problems that can occur when state banks are excluded from an analysis.[65]

James has added support to the Davis hypothesis of declining interest rate differences and added reasons for doubting the Davis and Sylla explanations of the decline. Concluding that neither the spread of the commercial paper dealers nor changes in the National Banking Act caused the decline, James left us with the impression that changes in state laws may have provided the explanation.

Indeed, the relative lack of study that was done for states or regions of the United States was surprising, in view of the great diversity in bank legal frameworks existing in this period. Even by 1913, most banks were chartered under widely divergent state laws. Of course the economies of the States also showed great divergences. Empirical investigation of the national economy, therefore, cannot be used to test the impact of a given bank structure on development, because the studies are actually of the effect of a particular collection of financial structures, rather than one structure. There were a large number of early, very descriptive studies and a few of these supply useable data. Margaret Myers' study of the New York money market was one source and R.M. Breckenridge provided material on discount rates for most important cities.[66]

Richard H. Keehn used the techniques of Davis and Sylla to study Wisconsin's banking structure in the late nineteenth century.[67] Keehn supplied a variety of information on Wisconsin banks. He presented information to test the hypothesis that the national banking laws inhibited bank entry, particularly in rural areas. Keehn showed that the number of banks in Wisconsin generally grew, although there was a setback in the period 1865-1880. By 1890 state banks were numerous and had larger assets than national banks. Keehn used an index of bank service developed by Cameron to show all counties had a high level of bank density throughout the period. Most counties also had more than $5.00 in bank deposits per person by 1900. The examination of bank formation led Keehn to conclude that where only one or two banks existed in a market, it was because of a small market rather than legal restrictions.

Since by 1900, deposit banking began to replace note issues and the capital requirements for state banks began to decline in some areas, it is possible that national banking became less profitable relative to state banks. To test this possibility Keehn calculated the ratio of profit to net worth. He found that national banking yielded a high return throughout the period of the national banking system. There was a very slight decline after 1900 in spite of the liberalized requirements for the national banks. Furthermore, periods which exhibited increasing profits coincided with periods of high bank entry rates.

Keehn attempted to compute interest rates in Wisconsin using the Davis techniques, and found the rates were higher than in eastern regions, although the difference declined over time. Country banks had higher rates than Milwaukee banks. This difference was not due to risk, as loss rates were lower for country banks. It may have been due to the capital requirement. Higher rates of return were probably necessary in the country banks to offset their lower asset to net worth ratios. Milwaukee banks each had an average of four to ten times the amount of assets held by each rural bank.

To determine whether economies of scale were important to nineteenth century banking, Keehn compared expenses to assets. He found scale economies were not important. He also attempted to consolidate some of his findings in a comprehensive model which predicted a bank's loan to asset ratio as a function of the number of banks in the market, the origin of the bank's charter, the amount of net worth, population, and percentage of time deposits.[68]

Keehn has also conducted studies of bank stock ownership and bank control in Wisconsin. His work has added to knowledge of the United States banking system and has stimulated other similar efforts,including my 1978 dissertation and a dissertation by Roger Lister both using California banks and a model very similar to Keehn's.[69]

More recently, Kerry Odell showed a healthy financial market existed on the West Coast of the United States, with the city of San Francisco constituting a regional version of New York. The development of this regional market over the years 1850 to 1920, she contended, hastened the development of a national capital market which emerged via linkage of the Pacific Coast with other regional markets.[70]

Except for the Lister and Pierson Doti dissertations, all of these studies of regions have used only national bank data to describe the banking system. There are many good reasons that state banks, savings banks and private banks also be included in such tests. As noted above these banks constituted the majority of banks in the United States. Omission of the state banks will tend to increase the bias in the results where the structure of the financial system is the issue. The difficulty suggested here stems from the inaccessibility of the information on state and private banks. Many states did not regularly collect information on the banks they chartered and the information that is available is in widely divergent format. Thus, empirical analysis will have to continue on a state-by-state basis.

The present study examines several issues in late nineteenth century banking theory and development using data from the California banking system. California has several advantages as a source of data. The state required all banks to report detailed balance sheets once or twice each year after 1878. California was still somewhat isolated from the rest of the country during the period, as were its financial markets. Yet the economy was large enough to permit studies of capital flows between sectors. Since banking laws and regulations were uniform throughout the state, financial shifts between sectors would not have been influenced by variations in banking law.

It is hoped that this study will make information on the banking system of one state easier to include in studies of the United States economy. The availability of state banking data would improve tests on the issues that remain unresolved. Including these banks can increase the accuracy of estimates of interest rate differentials and their movements. With complete information available on the California financial system, the state can be used to provide insight into the impact of a given financial structure on the development of an economy.

NOTES

1. Milton Friedman and Anna Jacobson Schwartz, *A Monetary History of the United States, 1867-1960* (Princeton: Princeton University Press, 1963).

2. The most concise treatment is in "The Quantity Theory of Money--A restatement" in *Studies in the Quantity Theory of Money*; ed. by Milton Friedman (Chicago: University of Chicago Press. 1956) pp. 3-21.

3. Philip Cagan, "The Monetary Dynamics of Hyper-inflation" in *Studies in the Quantity Theory of Money*, pp. 25-120.

4. *Ibid.*

5. Federal Reserve Bank of St. Louis, *Review* (Federal Reserve Bank, monthly).

6. Peter Temin, *Did Monetary Forces Cause the Great Depression?* (New York: W. W. Norton, 1976).

7. Alvin Hansen, *Cycles of Prosperity and Depression in the United States, Great Britain, and Germany* (Wisconsin: University of Wisconsin, Studies in the Social Sciences and History #5, 1921), pp. 104-108.

8. Wesley Mitchell, *Business Cycles: The Problem and its Setting* (New York: National Bureau of Economic Research, 1927), pp. 136-138.

9. Ludwig von Mises, *The Theory of Money and Credit.* (New Haven: Yale University Press, 1953. First printed in Germany, 1924). See p. 365.

10. R.G. Hawtrey, *Currency and Credit.* 2nd ed. (London: Longmans, Green and Co., 1923). See p. 10, also pp. 34-37.

11. Irving Fisher, *The Theory of Interest,* (New York: Macmillan Co., 1930).

12. Irving Fisher, *Booms and Depressions*, (New York: Adelphi, 1932).

13. John Maynard Keynes, *A Treatise on Money,* Vol. V (London: MacMillan for the Royal Economics Society, 1971).

14. John Maynard Keynes, *The General Theory of Employment Interest and Money*, (New York: Harcourt, Brace and World, Harbinger edition, 1964. First published 1936).

15. *Ibid.*, p. 82.

16. James E. Duesenberry, *Business Cycles and Economic Growth.* (New York: McGraw-Hill, 1958), pp. 321, 330.

17. See for example, John G. Gurley and Edward S. Shaw, "Financial Intermediaries and the Saving Investment Process." *Journal of Finance* 11 (May, 1956), pp. 265-273.

18. Philip Cagan, *The Channels of Monetary Effects on Interest Rates,* (New York: National Bureau of Economic Research, 1972.).

19. Bray Hammond, *Banks and Politics in America from the Revolution to the Civil War* (Princeton, N. J.: Princeton University Press, 1957).

20. George A. Selgin, *The Theory of Free Banking: Money Supply under Competitive Note Issue* (Totowa, NJ: Rowman and Littlefield, 1988); David Glasner, *Free Banking and Monetary Reform* (London:Cambridge University Press 1989); Lawrence White, *Free Banking in Britain: Theory, Experience, and Debate, 1800-1845* (New York: Cambridge University Press, 1984).

21. Larry J. Sechrest, *Free Banking: Theory, History, and a Laissez-Faire Model* (Westport CN: Quorum Books, 1993), p. 68; Milton Friedman, "The Role of Monetary Policy" *American Economic Review* 58 (March 1968), p. 12-14.

22. Henry M. Markowitz, *Portfolio Selection: Efficient Diversification of Investments,* (New Haven and London, Yale University Press, 1959). William Sharpe, *Portfolio Theory and Capital Markets,* (New York: McGraw-Hill, 1970). For other examples, see: Eugene F. Brigham and R. Richardson Pettit, "Effects of Structure on Performance in the Savings and Loan Industry," in *Study of the Savings and Loan Industry,* Vol. III by Irwin Friend, Federal Home Loan Bank Board (Washington D.C.: U.S. Government Printing Office, 1969), pp. 971-1211. Andrew Chen, "Optimal Bank Portfolio Management" in *Applications of Management Science in Banking and Finance,* ed by Samuel Eilson and Terence Fowles (Gower Press, 1972). Joel Fried, "Bank Portfolio Selection" *Journal of Financial Quantitative Analysis* 5 (June, 1970), pp. 203-227. Oliver Hart and Dwight M. Jaffee, "On the Application of Portfolio Theory to Depository Financial Intermediaries" *Review of Economic Studies* 41 (Jan., 1974), pp. 129-147. E.J. Kane and B.G. Malkiel, "Bank Portfolio Allocation, Deposit Variability and the Availability Doctrine," *Quarterly Journal of Economics* 79 (1965), pp. 113-134. George Morrison, *Liquidity Preferences of Commercial Banks,* (Chicago: University of Chicago Press, 1966). Richard Porter, "A Model of Bank Portfolio Selection," *Yale Economic Essays* 1 (Fall, 1961), pp. 323-359.

23. See Lionel I. Kalish and R. Alton Gilbert, "The Influence of Bank Regulation on the Operating Efficiency of Commercial Banks," *Journal of Finance* 28 (Dec., 1973), pp. 1287-1301, Their tests demonstrate no significant influence on current or potential competition in bank market on the operating efficiency of banks, p. 1288. Warren L. Smith in "Financial Intermediaries and Monetary Controls," *Quarterly Journal of Economics* 73 (Nov., 1959), pp. 533-553, contends financial intermediaries have not contributed much to the instability or ineffectiveness of monetary policy. John T. Emery in "Risk, Return and the Morphology of Commercial Banking," *Journal of Finance and Quantitative Analysis* 6 (March, 1971), pp. 763-782, concludes that regulations affect bank behavior when he found significant differences between profits of banks in different states. Numerous other studies concern themselves with this problem.

24. The literature on these areas is quite extensive. For examples of these studies, see David Alhadoff, *Monopoly and Competition in Banking*. (Berkeley, Calif.: University of California Press, 1954). Ernest Baltensperger, "Economies of Scale, Firm Size, and Concentration in Banking," 4 (Aug., 1972), pp. 467-488. Lyle Gramley, *A Study of Scale Economies in Banking* (Kansas City, Mo.: Federal Reserve Bank, 1962). Gary G. Gilbert and William Longbrake, "The Effects of Branching by Financial Institutions or Competition, Productive Efficiency and Stability: An Examination of the Evidence," *Journal of Bank Research* 4 (Winter, 1974), pp. 298-307, includes a bibliography.

25. Joseph A. Schumpeter, *The Theory of Economic Development: An Inquiry into Profits, Capital, Credit, Interest, and the Business Cycle*, (Cambridge, Mass,: Harvard University Press, 1951. Translated from the German second edition of 1926. The first edition was 1911), p. 71.

26. Alexander Gerschenkron, *Economic Backwardness in Historical Perspective*, (Cambridge, Mass.: Harvard University Press, 1962). Rondo Cameron, *Banking in the Early Stages of Industrialization: A Study In Comparative Economic History*. (New York: Oxford University Press, 1967), p. 304.

27. Raymond Goldsmith, *Financial Structure and Development*. (New Haven and London: Yale University Press, 1969), p. 390.

28. *Ibid.*, p. 44.

29. *Ibid.*, p. 391.

30. His major recent works on this theme are: Douglas North and Robert Paul Thomas, *Rise of the Western World*, (Cambridge: Cambridge University Press, 1973), and with Lance Davis, *Institutional Change and American Economic Growth*, (Cambridge: Cambridge University Press, 1971). The ideas presented here on the role of capital (see p. 28, 41, 109-125) parallel those of Davis in other works (see Bibliography).

31. John Jay Knox, *A History of Banking in the United States* (New York: Augustus M. Kelley, 1969. Originally published 1903). Forward by Bradford Rhodes, p. iii.

32. Paul B. Trescott, *Financing American Enterprise: The Story of Commercial Banking* (New York: Harper and Row, 1963).

33. Fritz Redlich, *The Molding of American Banking: Men and Ideas* (New York and London: Johnson Reprint Corp., 1968. Originally published, 1947), preface to second volume.

34. See Edward G. Bournes, *The History of the Surplus Revenue of 1837* (New York: Burt Franklin, 1885); Davis R. Dewey, State Banking before the Civil War (Washington, D.C.: Government Printing Office, 1910). Herman E. Kross and Martin R. Blyn, *A History of Financial Intermediaries* (New York: Random, 1971), although newer, is heavily influenced by older writers. Seel also Sister M. Grace Madeline, *Monetary and Banking Theories of Jacksonian Democracy* (Philadelphia: Kennika, 1970, Originally published 1943); Margaret G. Myers, *A Financial History of the United States* (New York and London: Columbia, 1970. Originally published 1931); James R. Sharp, *The Jacksonians vs. the Banks: Politics in the States after the Panic of 1837* (New York: Columbia University Printing Office, 1970); William Graham Summer, *A History of Banking in the United States* (New York: Augustus Kelley, 1971. Originally published 1896).

35. Richard Sylla, "American Banking and Growth in the Nineteenth Century: A Partial View of the Terrain" E*xplorations in Entrepreneurial History* 9 (Winter 1971-1972), p. 198.

36. Redlich, Vol. II, p. 8.

37. J. Van Fenstermaker, "The Statistics of American Commercial Banking 1782-1818," *Journals of Economic History* 25 (1965), p. 400. Peter Temin, "The Economic Consequences of the Bank War" *Journal of Political Economics* 76 (1968), pp. 227-274, and *The Jacksonian Economy* (U.S.A.: W.W. Norton, 1969). Hugh Rockoff, "The Free Banking Era: A Reexamination" (Ph.D. dissertation, University of Chicago, 1972). Summary Article of the same title, *Journal of Money,*

Credit and Banking 6 (May, 1974), p. 154. Also see Rockoff's "Money, Prices, and Banks in the Jacksonian Era," in R*einterpretation of American Economic History*, ed. by Robert Fogel and Stanley Engerman (New York: Harper and Row, 1971), pp. 448-458, and "Varieties of Banking and Regional Economic Development in the U.S., 1940-1860." *Journal of Economic History* 35 (March, 1975), pp. 160-181. Roger Hinderliter and Hugh Rockoff, "The Management of Reserves by Antebellum Banks in Eastern Financial Centers," *Explorations in Economic History* 11 (Spring, 1973), pp. 37-53.

38. Stanley Engerman, "A Note on the Economic Consequences of the Second Bank of the U.S." *Journal of Political Economy* 78 (July/August, 1970), pp. 725-728.

39. Rockoff, dissertation, p. 34-38.

40. Hinderliter and Rockoff.

41. Redlich, Vol. II, pp. 2-3.

42. Lance Davis, "The Investment Market, 1870-1914: The Evolution of a National Market," *Journal of Economic History* 25 (Sept 1965), pp. 355-399. Friedman & Schwartz include this period in *A Monetary History* and Philip Cagan amplifies their work in his *Determinants and Effects of Changes in the Stock of Money*, 1875-1960 (New York: National Bureau of Economic Research, 1965). Also see Cagan's article "The First Fifty Years of the National Bank Act-Historical Appraisal" in *Banking and Monetary Studies*, Diane Carson, ed. (Homewood, IL.: Richard D. Irwin, Inc., 1963).

43. Lance Davis, "The Investment Market, 1870-1914: *The Evolution of a National Market," Journal of Economic History* 25 (Sept. 1965), pp. 355-399. His regions coincide with Comptroller reports and are:
> Region I: Maine, Vermont, New Hampshire, Massachusetts, Connecticut, and Rhode Island.
> Region II: New York, New Jersey, Pennsylvania, Delaware, Maryland, and District of Columbia.
> Region III: Virginia, West Virginia, North Carolina, South Carolina, Florida, Alabama, Mississippi, Louisiana, Texas,

Arkansas, Kentucky, Tennessee, and Georgia.
Region IV: Ohio, Indiana, Illinois, Michigan, Wisconsin, Iowa, Minnesota, and Missouri.
Region V: North Dakota, South Dakota, Nebraska, Kansas, Montana, Wyoming, Colorado, New Mexico, and Oklahoma.
Region VI: Washington, Oregon, California, Idaho, Utah, Nevada, and Arizona.
Region 0: New York City

44. R.M. Breckenridge, "Discount Rates in the United States," *Political Science Quarterly* 13 (1898).

45. Davis, p. 380. From Comptroller's *Report*, 1890, I, p. 14.

46. Davis, p. 375. From G.K. Holmes and J.S. Lord "Report of Real Estate Mortgages in the United States," in *Eleventh Census of the United States Vol. XII* (Washington, 1895), pp. 4-5.

47. R.E. Severson, "The Sources of Mortgage Credit for Champaign County, 1865-1880," *Agriculture History*, 36 (July, 1962); J.Ladin, "The Sources of Mortgage Credit for Tippicanoe County 1865-1886 (unpublished); Allan Bogue, *Money at Interest* (Ithaca, N.Y.: Cornell University Press, 1955).

48. Davis, pp. 378-380.

49. Davis, pp. 392-393.

50. Richard Sylla, "Federal Policy, Banking Market Structure, and Capital Mobilization in the United States, 1863-1913," *Journal of Economic History* 19 (Dec., 1969), pp. 657-686.

51. Sylla, "Federal Policy," pp. 657-660.

52. Sylla, p. 680. From Margaret Myers, *The New York Money Market: Origins and Development* (New York: Columbia University Press, 1931), p. 236.

53. Gene Smiley, "Interest Rate Movement in the United States, 1888-1913," *Journal of Economic History* 35 (Sept., 1973), pp. 591-620.

54. Smiley, p. 597. His regions are:
I. Maine, Vermont, New Hampshire, Massachusetts, Connecticut, and Rhode Island.
II. New York, New Jersey, Pennsylvania, Delaware, Maryland, and the District of Columbia.
III-A. Virginia, West Virginia, North Carolina, Kentucky, and Tennessee.
III-B. South Carolina, Georgia, Florida, Alabama, Mississippi, Louisiana, Texas, Arkansas, and Oklahoma.
IV. Ohio, Indiana, Illinois, Michigan, Wisconsin, Minnesota, Iowa, and Missouri.
V. North Dakota, South Dakota, Nebraska, Kansas, Montana, Wyoming, Colorado, and New Mexico.
VI. Washington, Oregon, California, Idaho, Utah, Nevada, and Arizona.

55. Smiley, pp. 598-610.

56. John James, "Banking Market Structure, Risk, and the Pattern of Local Interest Rates in the United States 1893-1911," *Review of Economics and Statistics* 58 (November 1976), pp. 453-462.

57. *Ibid.*, p. 454.

58. William Sharpe and Hinderliter and Rockoff.

59. James, "Banking Market Structure," p. 455. The tested equation becomes
$R_t = a_1 CP_t + a_2 LS_t + a_3 LS_{t-1} + a_4 VAR_t + a_5 MP_t + a_6 BC_t + a_7 SEAS_t + a_8 + G_t$ where R_t is the average real quoted rate on commercial loans in period t using Warren-Pearson wholesale price index as a deflator.
CP_t is the real New York commercial paper rate.
LS_t is the loss rate on commercial loans.
VAR_t is the sample variance of the loss rate over the previous five years.

MP_t is the monopoly power index.
BC_t is the business cycle index in period t, the deviation from the trend of bank clearings outside New York City.
$SEAS_t$ is the seasonal dummy.

60. James, "Banking Market Structure," p. 461. See his article "A Note on Interest Paid on New York Bankers' Balances in the Postbellum Period" for his justification of the two percent figure. Although this article supports the contention that bankers received interest of two percent when depositing funds in New York, funds deposited as reserves in other banks probably did not receive that rate of interest.

61. James, "Banking Market Structure," p. 461; *F. Macauley, Some Theoretical Problems Suggested by the Movements of Interest Rates, Bond Yields, and Stock Prices in the United States Since 1856* (New York: National Bureau of Economic Research, 1938).

62. James uses the Cochrane-Orcutt technique, but even this improvement remains ineffective when there is autocorrelation compounded by lagged variables. See Robert Pindyck and Daniel Rubenfeld, *Econometric Models and Economic Forecasts* (McGraw-Hill, 1976), pp. 111-112; James L. Doti and Esmael Adibi, *Econometric Analysis: An Applications Approach* (Englewood Cliffs, New Jersey: Prentice Hall, 1988), pp. 257.

63. James, "Banking Market Structure," p. 459.

64. John James. "The Development of the National Money Market, 1893-1911)," *Journal of Economic History* 36 (December 1976), pp. 878-897.

65. James, "Development of the National Money Market" pp. 891-895. James attributes the decline in interest rate differences to decreases in the state capital requirement, but eight states on his list raised capital requirements between 1895 and 1909 versus eleven states decreasing their capital. Obviously, the question requires further study.

66. Margaret G. Myers, The New York Money Market, Origins and Development (New York: Columbia University Press, 1931). R.M. Breckenridge "Discount Rates in the United States," *Political Science Quarterly* 13 (1898), p. 119.

67. Richard H. Keehn, "Federal Bank Policy, Bank Market Structure, and Bank Performance: Wisconsin, 1863-1914." *Business History Review* 48 (Spring, 1974). Also see his "Market Structure and Bank Performance: Wisconsin, 1870-1900" (Ph.D. dissertation, University of Wisconsin, 1971), "Bank Stock Ownership and Bank Control: The Evidence from Wisconsin, 1860-1900" paper presented at the Business History Conference, Northwestern University, IL., February 28-March 1, 1975.

68. Richard H.Keehn, "Bank Market Structure and Individual Bank Performance: Some Evidence from Wisconsin, 1870-1900," paper presented at the Western Economic Association Conference, San Diego, California, June 25-28, 1975, pp. 10-13.

69. Roger Lister, "Market Structure and Economic Performance: California Banking; 1890-1900," paper presented at the Western Economic Association meetings, Anaheim, California, June 21, 1977; dissertation published as *Bank Behavior, Regulation, and Economic Development California, 1860-1910* (New York:Garland,1993); Lynne Pierson Doti, "Banking in California, Some Evidence on Structure 1878-1905" (Ph.D. thesis, University of California Riverside, 1978).

70. Kerry Odell, *Capital Mobilization and Regional Financial Markets: The Pacific Coast States, 1850-1920* (New York: Garland Publishing, Inc., 1992).

II

EARLY HISTORY OF CALIFORNIA BANKING

Rules and regulations of the national banking system, the laws of other states concerning banking; and the economic and political history of California all influenced the behavior of state bankers. The few banking laws which were enacted in California during this era may have had some impact as well.

THE NATIONAL BANKING SYSTEM AND STATE BANKS

In the period under study the Federal government was chartering banks under the National Banking Act of 1864, while each state chartered its banks under widely divergent laws. The total number of national banks was about twenty-one hundred in 1880 and about five thousand by 1905.[1] There were roughly five hundred state banks at the beginning of the period and ten thousand at the end of the period.[2]

National Banks had minimum capital requirements, note issue restricted by the bank's holdings of government bonds, and limits on their lending, with specific directions about diversification of their asset portfolio. They were not allowed to lend on real estate. State banks generally had less stringent requirements. The National Bank capital requirements was $50,000 until 1900 when it decreased to $25,000 for some rural areas. Most states required between ten and twenty-five thousand dollars of capital by the end of the period, although several states still had no minimum in 1905. In those states where minimum capital subscription was required, the method of timing of payment was often lenient enough to nullify the impact of the requirement.[3] Note issue of National Banks was limited by the requirement that the issue could not exceed ninety percent of the par value of bonds deposited with the U.S. Treasury, or the capital stock of the bank. Most governments state also limited note circulation by some technique. Establishing a ratio between notes in circulation and capital, surplus, and dividends was common. Many states did not allow note issue within their borders. The federal tax of ten percent also discouraged the issue of state bank notes.

The prohibition of loans on real estate by national banks formed one of the most characteristic differences between state and national banks, although there are indications that national banks avoided the impact of this restriction.[4] A few states limited the amount of lending on real estate, but none prohibited it entirely.[5]

National banks could not loan more than an amount equal to ten percent of its capital stock to any one borrower. State bank laws also usually limited the amount of a bank's assets that could be loaned to any one party. The limit was uniformly stated as a percentage of the capital accounts and ranged, by 1905, from ten percent of capital plus surplus and undivided profit to thirty percent of capital plus surplus. In only two of the states was the amount a bank could loan to one person certainly less than what could be loaned by a national bank.[6] Both state and national banks could exceed the limits for loans when the borrower offered strong collateral.[7]

Reserve requirements were another method of restricting banking activity. The national banks' graduated system, which based reserves upon location, was duplicated by few states. Only four states based reserves entirely on location. Most states used the type of deposit to determine the reserve requirement. The national banks required between fifteen and twenty-five percent reserves. The state requirements by 1910 ranged from ten to twenty-five percent, although about ten states had no reserve requirements and California had just enacted a reserve requirement that was only four percent on time deposits (fifteen percent on demand deposits).[8]

Bank examination was another requirement that was more stringent for national banks than for state banks. National banks were required to supply reports on their condition annually and were examined by the Comptroller of the Currency. Only four states required regular examination by 1887, but most states had initiated this requirement by 1910.[9]

From these comparisons, it is apparent that some incentive was necessary to gain recruits for the National Banking System. The incentive was partly provided by the federally imposed tax on state bank notes, but this tax apparently provided only a temporary disincentive to state bank creation. There were almost eleven hundred state banks when the tax was initiated in 1864. Four years later, the number had declined to two hundred and fifty. The number grew rapidly thereafter. The declining importance of bank notes as a means of raising funds is generally cited as the reason state banks recovered their important position.[10]

NINETEENTH CENTURY BANKING THEORY

Banking theorists had quite divergent ideas during the late nineteenth century about what makes for a healthy financial system and their ideas explain a variety of the laws of the time. One tenet of banking thought was the commercial loan theory. The essence of this theory is that banks should confine themselves to discounting short term "self-liquidating" commercial bills because their liabilities are short term. The cornerstones of the theory are species reserves adequate to meet liabilities and ample capital to allow for the possibilities of bad assets.[11]

A second tenet of banking thought that was strong during this period was free banking, in the sense of unrestricted banking activity. Free banking is associated with early mercantilist philosopher, Sir James Stewart. A more contemporary American prophet was Alexander Bryan Johnson, who felt that bank expansion had a natural limit: loans would only be requested if there are sufficient projects which will be profitable.[12] Free banking had various degrees of advocacy, ranging from the federalist historian Richard Hildreth's view that "capitalists must be felt as much at liberty to invest their money in a bank as in a cotton mill,"[13] to the more generally held feelings that, aside from note issue, bank activities were to be encouraged.

Bank theorists of the day knew that banks could expand the money supply,[14] and felt this elasticity was an important feature of a healthy economy.[15] The United States still had a relatively unsophisticated financial sector. The common man in many parts of the country was reluctant to demand the services of financial institutions. Those men who carried on financial activities were generally among the economic leaders of their communities and therefore were often influential in political matters. In banking legislation the direction of their influence was not decisive. They naturally wished little restraint upon their own activities, but wished much more restraint upon their rivals'. As noted, the resulting legislation was not overly restrictive, so the first desire may have been the stronger.

CALIFORNIA BANKING

Before the California Board of Bank Commissioners was established in 1878, little information was published about banking activity. The state was new and unsettled. There probably were not a lot of bankers, or they may have been wary of releasing information. Whatever the reason, there were no bankers' publications, and the government did not solicit information.[16]

The banking situation from 1878 to 1905 was, of course, shaped by earlier history.[17] California's rapid transition from Mexico's remote trading outpost to one of the United States' most important frontier areas occurred with stunning rapidity. As an isolated economy, California had little need of financial institutions. Cattle hides and other pelts constituted the bulk of the money supply into the 1840's.[18] Gold, silver and a wide variety of foreign coin served as "small change."[19] In the Spanish era, from the founding of the first mission in 1769 to Mexican independence in 1821, the missions served as trading posts for export products of vast ranches that dotted the state, but these ranches were largely self-sufficient domains with little need for cash. The Mexican government ousted the Catholic church in 1835 and California was left to gather settlers like John Sutter, a Swiss-born misfit who came to rule his own empire.[20]

The gold rush of 1848, started by a discovery on Sutter's land, established gold, traded by weight, as the currency for Californians. In the early years other money still circulated. Gold miners accepted eastern United States bills for their gold and gave them limited circulation in anticipation of the fact that they would return to the East after their fortune was made.[21] However, the isolation from the United States and the fact that many of the miners were from other countries meant U.S.paper money was heavily discounted, and gold became the currency of choice.

In spite of the preference for gold, banks opened almost immediately in San Francisco, the port of entry for those gold-seekers arriving from the sea, and in Sacramento, the inland river port town where miners replenished their supplies before heading up to the gold-filled hills. Ira Cross, in his definitive 1927 history, credits Robert A. Parker of San Francisco with serving as the first banker in town. He probably offered banking services in 1848 as a corollary to his store.[22] In 1849, at least six banks operated in San Francisco. Most of the early bankers were exchange dealers, offering certificates of deposit or other types of notes in return for gold. Gold prices in California ranged from $8 to $16 per ounce while gold the bankers shipped to New York was sold for $18. The early banks also offered loans and "borrowed" gold from customers.[23] The notes issued by early banks were denominated for as little as 25 cents: the standard price of a shot of whisky - equivalent to a pinch of gold dust. Such currency simplified transactions. Pinches were, after all, relative things, and quality of gold was so important that merchants had to learn to distinguish the source of the gold they took in payment. In fact, coining was a popular private enterprise until even after the U.S. mint was established in 1854.[24]

CALIFORNIA BANKING LAW

The discovery of gold was almost coincident with the cession of California to the United States, before any legal system or government was established,[25] so laws governing the activities of financial institutions were not the result of careful thought and experience. The first legislation relating to banking, in fact, was the state constitution.

Incorporation of banks was the first hotly debated issue at the constitutional convention of 1849.[26] The majority opinion was that banking activities should be limited to private individuals.[27] The California Constitution, written in haste, was based on the state constitution of Iowa and New York, with concessions to the treaty with Mexico. The part relating to bank activities in the version submitted to the convention was similar to the wording in New York's constitution in prohibiting special legislative charters.[28] However, there was a very strong group, including the prominent politician William Gwin, which touted the dangers of allowing banks at all. Stirred by personal experience, Gwin and others described the evils of paper money and wildcat banks.[29] But most delegates had experienced the disadvantages of gold and felt the depositing gold and receiving paper receipts was an indispensable practice. The New York wording was altered to maintain individual liability for corporate debt.[30]

After several days of heated debate among the delegates, a compromise was reached. The resulting sections relating to banking were finalized as:[31]

Article IV
Section 34: No association may issue paper to circulate as money.
Section 35: No person can act as a bank or circulate money.

There is little doubt that the provision against banks was immediately violated and rarely enforced. John Jay Knox described a bank established in 1848 that operated on two hundred thousand dollars of capital.[32] Ira Cross dates the first California banks from about 1849.[33]

Another ineffectual bank law was passed in 1850. The ceiling on interest rates was established at ten percent per year, with the proviso that, on special contracts, any rate of interest could be agreed and paid.[34] Interest rate in this period were closer to ten percent per month,[35] and the Miner's bank is said to have charged eight to fifteen percent.[36] By 1860 the rates seem to have declined to two or three percent per month,[37] but they did not reach ten percent a year for several decades.

Other legislation slowly paved the way to acceptance and regulation of all banking activities except note issue. In 1853, the Legislature passed an act to license bankers and financial brokers. The price of the license was based on the dollar volume of transactions that involved the sale or transmittance of bills of exchange, notes or bonds, gold or silver, or on the dollar volume of loans. The tax was reduced in 1854 and activities were separated into that of brokerage (dealing with stocks, securities, and gold) and banking (issuing bills of exchange and drafts).[38]

California bankers' ability to freely engage in branch banking throughout its history is almost unique in the United States. Modern theory is decisive on the positive impact of branching, although proponents of restricted branching argue that such restrictions are essential to prevent dominance by a few large institutions and to maintain and protect the viability of small local institutions which are presumed to be more responsive to community needs.[39] It is obvious that if economies of scale are an important factor, the ability to open branches might allow banks in any location to expand to acquire the advantage of lower cost.[40] Banks with branches in several areas also acquire the benefits of diversity in their portfolios of assets. Until the 1980s, the most widely accepted view of branching was that loosening restrictions on branch banking would cause the number of banks to decline, the number of offices to increase, and the mean total asset size of banks to increase.[41] Based on observation of the 1920s and 1960s California experience, the effect is temporary.[42] There are some proponents of the viewpoint that branching increases competition. Starting a new bank requires an investment in capital stock. A market must be large enough to warrant this fixed cost. But if branching is allowed an established bank can open a branch without new capital. It could operate with limited services by referring some customers to the parent bank. As the area grows, more services can be added.[43] In other words the financial needs of a rural community might only be met if branch banking is allowed.

Certainly the fact that branching is allowed would have a minimal effect where there are few barriers to opening a new bank. As this was the case in nineteenth century California, the fact that branching was allowed probably did not cause the financial structure to differ greatly from other states with few restrictions on banking. As a practical consideration, it is difficult to isolate the effects of branching in California. The branches each reported as individual banks, and, most importantly, branching was not widespread in the nineteenth century.[44]

After a rash of bank failures in 1855, a law was passed to strengthen the injunction against issuing currency. The first offense was a misdemeanor bringing a maximum sentence of three months in jail plus a two thousand dollar fine. The second offense became a felony which could bring up to five years imprisonment.[45] But banking continued to develop without note issue. At least one San Francisco bank claims to have incorporated under the general incorporation laws in 1857,[46] and Cross agrees there were several incorporated banks by 1860.[47]

In 1862, savings banks were exempted from the 1850 prohibition against banking firms and specifically allowed to incorporate. In 1864, savings banks with a minimum of $300,000 capital were permitted to carry on commercial activities.[48] After 1862, banks freely incorporated under either the general incorporation laws or the savings bank incorporation law.[49] In the 1879 revision of the state constitution the banking sections were dropped. These incorporation practices played a part in blurring the distinction between commercial and savings banks, so both are combined for this study. Both types carried term and ordinary deposits and they loaned on similar security.[50] Even the names of the bank confuse the distinction.

The first National Gold Banks in the United States were opened in California in 1872 after Congress created notes payable only in gold coin to allow the note-shy Californians to participate in the National Banking System.[51] Ten banks in California were chartered under this provision, but became regular national banks when the laws changed again in 1879. This same resistance to bank notes meant National Banks did not achieve a strong position in California until late in this period. Even by 1900, there were only thirty-five national banks in California.[52] The number almost doubled in the first ten years after the requirements for rural banks were changed in 1900, and most of these new banks located in the southern portion of the state as growth accelerated there.[53]

BANKING IN THE 1870s

The 1870s decade brought depression and disruption of the California economy. Speculation had over-inflated land prices in anticipation of completion of the transcontinental railroad. Unemployment rose when workers left the project and came to the coast.[54] It was also the decade when the balance between farming and cattle ranching shifted in favor of the farmer,[55] and the once-legendary production of the Comstock Silver Lode declined. A rash of bank failures marked the period, the first being the closing of the Bank of California in August, 1875.

The San Francisco clearing house began operations in 1876 with fifteen members. Five more banks joined by July, 1877, by which time $476,123,237.97 had been cleared by US Treasury gold certificates and gold coin.[56] This is the earliest banking organization and source of banking information for California.

Benjamin C. Wright, a California historian, is a source for some information on the banks in California for the seventies. He constructed a list of all banks in existence; their capital; deposits and cash on hand for July 1, 1876; and added further information for another report for December, 1876.[57]

In spite of Wright's efforts, regularly published data on California banks is not available until after Banking Act of March, 1878. This act had several provisions. It created a Board of Bank Commissioners, required all banks to pay a license fee, file reports, and be examined twice yearly. Only four New England states, Indiana, and Iowa preceded California in the examination requirement.[58] Three examiners were hired at salaries of $3,000 per year and immediately commenced their examinations.[59] The early results were not comforting. The first examined bank was closed by the examiners. The second passed inspection, but the next three all closed without repaying their depositors in full. Three of the four closed banks were among the largest in the state, having a combined total of nearly nine million dollars of deposits.[60] Bankers promptly went to court to prevent further examinations, claiming the new board had jurisdiction only over banks incorporated under the savings bank law of 1862. Their case failed and the commissioners continued examinations, with more favorable results.[61]

One prominent historian claims the railroad interests controlled the state bank commission.[62]

> A banker who gave aid and comfort to the railroad's enemies could suddenly find himself in disastrous trouble with the board of commissioners. Consequently, a businessman or a farmer who displeased the railroad by denouncing its rates, or by voting gate to a party convention, or by opposing its measures while serving as a member of the legislature, would suddenly find himself unable to obtain further loans from his bank.

BANKING IN THE 1880s AND 1890s

In the first decade during which the state banks were examined, the gold industry declined, the wine industry was fighting a lethal pest, and the citrus industry began and finally stretched from San Bernardino to San Diego and Pasadena to Riverside. Wheat was still the primary crop, but other agricultural activities were soon to exceed its importance. Two events marked financial history. In 1887, the state required private banks to file reports and Los Angeles bankers formed a clearing house.[63]

California did not feel the impact of the early nineties depression as fully as did eastern states. Seven banks failed in the worst year, 1893, while 598 banks failed in the rest of the country.[64] The California economy was generally healthy, with oil discoveries adding a new industry.

In 1895, the state required that all banking corporations have a minimum capital of $25,000.[65] The same year, the California Supreme Court found commercial banks were not forbidden to lend on real estate and interpreted the 1850 constitution as meaning to prohibit only paper currency, not banking.[66]

The Board had continued its examinations and reports twice a year while complaining frequently of the great inconvenience of the task. In 1898, the Legislature heeded their pleas and allowed annual examination.

THE END OF THE UNREGULATED ERA

The 1878 Banking Act was suspended in 1903 and quickly replaced with a very similar law which was amended extensively in 1905. The 1905 act initiated a reserve requirement for commercial banks, made bank examination optional for the commissioners, required licenses of private bankers, allowed the state to deposit funds in banks and instituted capital requirements of $25,000 to $100,000, dependent on city size. This last provision was declared unconstitutional and was replaced in 1907 with a statute requiring a minimum of $25,000 capital or ten percent of total liabilities up to $100,000 maximum.[67]

In 1909, the banking law was completely rewritten and the Board of Bank Commissioners was replaced with a State Superintendent of Banks. Capital requirements were increased and made partially dependent upon location. A reserve requirement was initiated and a large number of detailed requirements concerning the asset portfolio were written.[68] Unregulated banking had become a part of California's history.

NOTES

1. Board of Governors of the Federal Reserve System, *Banking Studies* (Washington, D.C., 1941), p. 418.

2. George Ernest Barnett, *State Banks and Trust Companies Since the Passage of the National Banking Act* (National Monetary Commission, Vol. 11, 61st Congress 3rd session, document number 659. Government Printing Office, 1911), p. 200 shows estimates of the number of state banks.

3. Barnett, pp. 36-37, summarized state capital requirements; p. 54 states that the amount of capital paid up was left to the discretion of the bank's officers.

4. Richard Keehn and G. Smiley, "Mortgage Lending by National Banks, 1890-1914," presented at the Western Economic Association meetings, San Francisco, California, June, 1976.

5. Barnett, p. 99.

6. *Ibid.*, p. 88 gives details of state's requirements.

7. *Ibid.*, p. 89.

8. *Ibid.*, pp. 112-113.

9. *Ibid.*, p. 148.

10. Lester V. Chandler, *The Economics of Money and Banking,* 6th ed. (New York: Harper and Row, 1973), p. 100.

11. Richard Sylla, "American Banking and Growth in the Nineteenth Century: A Partial View of the Terrain." *Explorations in Economic History* 9 (Winter 1971-72), pp. 202-203.

12. *Ibid.*, p. 203.

13. Richard Hildreth, *The History of Banks: To Which is added a Demonstration of the Advantages and Necessity of Free Competition in the Business of Banking* (New York: Augustus M. Kelley, 1968, pp. 108-110. Originally published in 1837).

14. Lloyd Mints, *A History of Banking Theory* (Chicago: University of Chicago Press, 1945), p. 200.

15. *Ibid.*, p. 223.

16. Leroy Armstrong and J.O. Denny, *Financial California: A Historical Review of the Beginnings and Progress of Banking in the State* (San Francisco: The Coast Banker Publishing Co., 1916), p. 14.

17. For a more complete history of banking in California, see Lynne Pierson Doti and Larry Schweikart, *California Bankers 1848-1993* (Needham Heights, MA: Ginn Press, 1994).

18. Ira B. Cross, *Financing an Empire: History of Banking in California*, 4 volumes (Chicago, San Francisco, Los Angeles: S.J. Clarke Publishing Co., 1927) pp. 22-23 (Vol.I). The famous Sutter's Mill was paid for with installments of wheat, soap and furs.

19. Benjamin Wright, *Banking in California, 1849-1910* (San Francisco: H.S. Crocker Co., 1910), p. 8.

20. Cross, p. 22.

21. Armstrong, p. 15.

22. Cross, *Financing an Empire*, p. 44.

23. Cross, p. 40.

24. The Smithsonian has an extensive collection of privately minted California gold coins.

25. Military rule established after the cession continued until California was accepted for statehood in 1850.

26. David Alan Johnson, *Founding the Far West: California, Oregon and Nevada, 1840-1890* (Berkeley: University of California Press, 1992), p. 122.

27. Armstrong, p. 18.

28. *Ibid.*, p. 82.

29. Johnson, p. 123.

30. Walter Bean, *California, An Interpretive History* (New York and San Francisco: McGraw-Hill, 1968), p. 200.

31. Armstrong, p. 18.

32. John Jay Knox, *A History of Banking in the United States* (New York: Augustus M. Kelley, 1969), p. 843. Originally published in 1903). Refers to Miner's bank.

33. See Cross, pp. 39-41. He also mentions Miner's Bank.

34. Armstrong, p. 84.

35. Wright, p. 158.

36. Knox, p. 843.

37. Wright, p. 156. Armstrong says interest rates were down to 3% a month by 1853, p. 82.

38. Armstrong, p. 74-75.

39. Gary Gilbert and William Longbrake, "Part II, The Effects of Branching by Financial Institutions on Competition, Productive Efficiency, and Stability: An Examination of the Evidence," *Journal of Bank Research* 4 (Winter 1974), p. 156.

40. Ernest Baltensperger, "Economics of Scale, Firm Size, and Concentration in Banking," *Journal of Money, Credit and Banking* 4 (August 1972), p. 478.

41. See for instance, Donald Jacobs, "The Interaction Effects of Restrictions on Branching and Other Bank Regulations," *Journal of Finance* 20 (May 1965), pp. 332-349. R.F. Lanzellotti and T.R. Savings, "State Branching Restrictions and the Availability of Branching Services: A Comment," *Journal of Money, Credit and Banking 1* (November 1969), p. 786, indicates branching restrictions do not result in fewer bank offices.

42. Lynne Pierson Doti, "Nationwide Branching: Some Lessons from California," *Essays in Business and Economic History* (Economic and Business Historical Society, 1991).

43. Jacobs illustrates this process.

44. Cross suggests this fact, p. 913, and examination of bank reports reveals that there are only a few banks with the same name in any one year. Knox, p. 196, states that only five branches existed in the state in 1905. Of course, shortly after the period studied here, A.P. Giannini embarked upon his famous career and by 1927 had 279 branches of the Bank of Italy, located in every part of the state (Cross, p. 911).

45. *Ibid.*, p. 76.

46. Wright, p. 102.

47. Cross, p. 152. Armstrong says the 1850 prohibition of banking was void by 1864, p. 77.

48. Armstrong, p. 19.

49. *Ibid.*, p. 22.

50. Knox, p. 850, says there was little difference between the two. The Board of Bank Commissioners makes the distinction based only upon the incorporation laws. If the bank was incorporated under the 1862

Savings Bank Act, it was classified as a savings bank. Otherwise, it was a commercial bank. Examination of bank names and data in their reports confirms the similarity of the two types.

51. Knox, p. 845. Also see p. 112. Ira Cross, p. 97. states his opinion that Californians were reluctant to accept any type of paper currency until the first World War.

52. Wright, pp. 90-93, gives details of the number in each year.

53. *Ibid.*, p. 99, notes that seventy-two of the one hundred seventy-six national banks with less than $50,000 capital were located in California. Examination of the bank reports locates these mostly in Southern California.

54. Bean, pp. 219-220.

55. *Ibid.*, p. 205.

56. Wright, p. 105, provides information on the opening and early activity. Armstrong, p. 159, gives method of payment.

57. *Ibid.*, p. 125.

58. Armstrong, p. 23.

59. The National Bank examiners were paid a fee based on the number of examinations. Wright, p. 130.

60. *Ibid.*, p. 108.

61. Frank LeRoy Kidner, *California Business Cycles* (Berkeley and Los Angeles, University of California Press, 1946), p. 26.

62. Bean, pp. 305-6.

63. Cross, p. 885.

64. Wright, p. 110.

65. Barnett, p. 37, claims there were not many banks where the capital was less than $25,000.

66. Armstrong, p. 20.

67. Cross, p. 676.

68. *Ibid.*, pp. 719-728.

III

THE COMPETITIVE BANKING ENVIRONMENT

The history of California banking described in the previous section suggests there was minimal government interference in the allocation of capital. This leads one to expect the capital market would have operated in a competitive manner, unless other factors reduced competition. Before discussing these other factors, the model of perfect competition will be examined.

BANK BEHAVIOR IN A COMPETITIVE MARKET

The firm in a perfectly competitive market has a minimal influence on the price of the product it sells because of the large number of other firms willing to sell the identical product. If economic profit were to increase, additional production would quickly occur and the extra supply would lower the price until extra-normal profits were bid away. Price will be just equal to the minimum average total cost of producing the good or service.

If banking is a perfectly competitive industry, there are several characteristics that would be observed. All firms would charge the same price because a firm attempting to charge a higher price would find all of the customers frequenting his rivals' firms. They would charge the same interest rate on each particular type of loan. In this perfectly competitive model they would also pay the same interest on deposits received, because buyers would stop for the highest interest paid on deposits. As a new geographic area developed with a new, more profitable use for capital, interest rates everywhere would rise. The increased demand for capital created by the new use would allow bankers in the area to charge higher interest. Bankers in other areas would transfer capital to the new area so they, too, could receive higher interest. This would lead to scarcity of capital in the old areas and this shortage would cause interest rates in the old areas to rise while interest rates in the new area were declining due to the extra supply. Interest rates in different locations would thus tend to be equalized.

An alternate situation was described by Sylla in his 1969 article. He hypothesized that the National Banking Laws restricted the number of banks in areas where the population was scattered, which discouraged capital from moving into rural areas and created a two-tiered financial market in the United States. The banks in large cities were in a competitive capital market which operated as described by the perfectly competitive model. The rural banker operated as a price-discriminating monopolist. A price-discriminating monopolist of the third degree separates his customers into groups which each have different elasticities of demand for his product. Possibilities for resale of the product between groups must be eliminated. The producer then determines his profit maximizing output and allocates it between markets by equating marginal cost to marginal revenue in each market. If the marginal revenue in one market were greater than in the other market, profit could be increased by allocating less output to the second market to allocate more to the first market.

To see this, consider figure 1. The producer will choose the output where the marginal cost of his entire output is equal to the common value of the marginal revenue in the two markets. The profit maximizing output is Q, where MR is the sum of the two marginal revenue curves. This output is then distributed between the two markets, with OQ1 to market 1 and OQ2 to market 2. Market 2 with the greater, more inelastic demand will be charged the higher price P2 while the same good is sold at P1 in the first market.[1] Sylla portrayed the rural banker as having two customers, the local potential borrowers, and the city bankers who sought his deposits. The demand curve from the city banks was perfectly elastic. The amount of funds any one country banker transferred to the city was very small relative to the overall amount of funds in the city and therefore had no impact on the price. In other words, the city banker paid some constant interest rate for the funds deposited by the country banker.

FIGURE 1

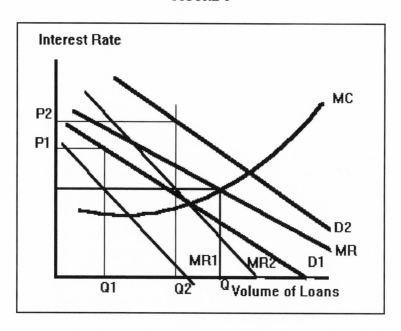

D1	demand for market 1
D2	demand for market 2
MR	marginal revenue for D1 + D2
MR1	marginal revenue for D1
MR2	marginal revenue for D2
MC	marginal cost
Q	total quantity produced
Q1	quantity sold to market 1
Q2	quantity sold to market 2
P1	price to market 1 buyers
P2	price to market 2 buyers

In the rural market the banker was a monopolist in his own community. The markets were separated, city bankers could not or would not resell the capital to rural customers. The rural banker might also have been able to distinguish between customers within the rural market. Figure 2 illustrates the situation portrayed in this Sylla model. D1 is the demand by the rural borrowers, D2 is the demand by the city banks and also the total marginal revenue of loans to the city. In the simpler case where there is no discrimination between rural borrowers, the rural bank produces OQ3 and allocates OQ1 of this to the rural market at an interest rate OP1. The remainder of the output, OQ3 - OQ1 is deposited in city banks at an interest rate of OP2. Interest rates in the cities will be less than rural rates. If the monopolist can discriminate perfectly between rural borrowers, as well as dividing his market into urban or rural classes, he will increase his amount loaned to rural borrowers to OQ2 since ACD2 becomes his marginal revenue curve. The remaining output, OQ3 - OQ2 is allocated to city bank deposits. The city interest rate will be OP2 but rural average interest rates will be higher. Only interest on the last dollar lent in the rural market will equal the city bank interest rate. It should be noted that Sylla's model would not allow us to perceive the existence of monopoly power on the basis of quantity tests alone. The discriminating monopolist did not necessarily produce less rural lending than a perfectly competitive firm.

FIGURE 2

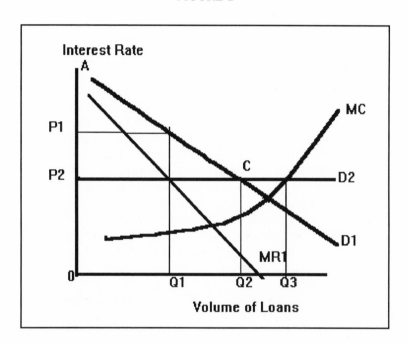

D1	demand curve for rural market
D2	demand curve for urban banks
MR1	marginal revenue curve for D1
MC	marginal cost
Q1	quantity sold in the rural market when there is no discrimination between rural borrowers
Q2	total amount of funds available for loans to rural borrowers when there is perfect discrimination between rural borrowers
Q3	total amount of funds available for loans
P1	interest received from rural borrowers
P2	interest received from city banks

According to Sylla the creation of rural monopolies was a result of the high capital requirements for national banks which made entry difficult. Rural areas often could not provide sufficient deposits to achieve a profitable capital to asset ratio. A tax on state bank notes and the absence of branch banking also prevented state banks from expanding sufficiently to create a competitive market. Rural depositors supposedly did not find deposit banking a viable substitute for bank notes, although sophisticated city dwellers accepted the lack of bank notes. Presumeably, the urban dwellers were more impressed by the higher interest on deposits banks could pay to avoid the tax.

These factors did not seem to apply in the California case. National banking was clearly restricted in the state. It is possible that the high capital requirement discouraged their formation. The rapid increase in the number of national banks in the state after 1900 supports this view. However, the necessity of accepting national bank notes was often cited as a reason for the scarcity of national banks in California. With the almost total lack of government restraint on state banking, state banks should have been able to expand to fill any gaps in the coverage of the capital market. Since California distrusted bank notes, it is less likely that the federal tax on their issue impeded the spread of state banks.

Even though few restrictions seemed to be present which would have created a monopoly situation in California, interest rates would probably still not show complete uniformity over the state; there are factors other than government interference which cause interest rates to differ. Financial institutions operate by issuing financial claims upon themselves in order to acquire funds to secure financial claims on others.[2] They exist because of information and transaction costs, risk, and economies of scale. Investors purchasing financial assets must first obtain knowledge about the issuer of the security, and evaluate the safety of the investment. In making the investment, there are further expenses incurred in time, paperwork or broker's fees. Further, investors are generally risk-averse. That is, they prefer less risk to more. Risk can be reduced by foregoing earnings or by diversification of holdings. Most securities are imperfectly divisible, so diversification is most easily achieved with larger pools of funds.[3] Large portfolios also bring the investor liquidity because of offsetting fluctuation in the value of assets. The brokers' fees will also be less per unit with larger investments.

The economies of scale allow a financial intermediary to develop to collect the funds of many investors into a larger pool. The reduction in unit costs of acquiring a portfolio allows a profit margin for the intermediary. The financial intermediary develops by issuing secondary claims against itself to break down the portfolio into less expensive and more liquid units.[4] Without these economies of scale, financial intermediaries would not exist.[5]

If the raison d'etre for financial institution's existence is economics of scale, it is quite possible that monopoly will exist in the industry. If the average cost of collecting funds and reinvesting reaches a minimum at a scale that is adequate to supply the entire market at a profitable set of prices with only one firm, there will exist a natural monopoly. If more than one firm exists in the market each firm would be inclined to cut its price to gain an increased share of the market. The resulting higher output would mean lower costs. Only one firm would survive if there were some isolated areas where the market was too small for even one bank to achieve a size that allowed it to produce at minimum average cost. Figure 3 shows how a bank in this situation would operate. Output would be Q1 and the price would be P1. As the market increased in size, more banks would be able to enter into competition and eventually the price would fall to P2.[6]

FIGURE 3

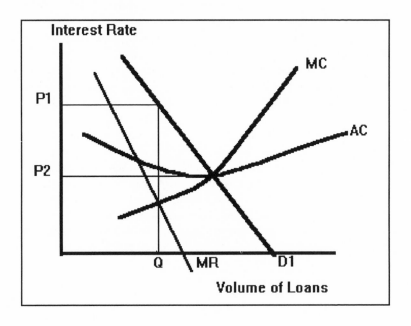

D1	rural demand
MR	rural marginal revenue
AC	average total cost
MC	marginal cost
Q	monopolist's output
P1	monopolist's price
P2	competitive price

EFFICIENT MARKETS

If the city market had sufficient competition to be considered a perfect market and country bankers had insufficient demand to achieve minimum cost, a difference in interest rates would exist. However, these differences should not exceed the cost of transferring funds from the city banks to country borrowers. If the difference was greater, city bankers would transfer some of their lending to rural borrowers. This would increase the funds available in the rural market, causing a decrease in price, and decrease funds available in the urban market, raising prices there.

There may be barriers to this transfer of funds from one area to another. Government intervention has been used to block the flow of funds. Throughout the history of the United States, the state and federal governments have erected a wide variety of barriers to free competition between bankers. The methods have ranged from prohibiting all banking activity within the state, limiting or prohibiting note issue (once bankers' main source of funds), limits on opening new banks, to the prohibition of branches.[7]

VARIATION IN THE COSTS FOR BANKERS

As stated earlier, California had few government imposed restrictions. But there still could be variations in interest rates without monopoly. Whether or not the absence of monopoly is a sufficient condition for a market to be considered competitive is controversial, but it conveys the desired message; interest rates differentials will decline eventually to the difference in cost of serving the markets.[8] These differences in cost, however, are themselves barriers to entry. There are two main areas where this may be relevant. The first of these is risk. Even in a perfect capital market, local interest rates may diverge if differences in risk exist. Monopoly and risk may be interrelated. Banks in a high risk area may be able to maintain a high price because the high risk of local loans makes entry unattractive.[9] It would be unreasonable to consider differences in interest rates due to difference in risk market imperfections. All banks attempting to serve the risky market will charge higher rates. Those banks less unwilling to assume risk will charge a lower premium and would service the riskier areas.[10]

While it is certainly not relevant for financial products today, one cost of trade has long been recognized in the literature. This is transportation cost. In an efficient market there will be only one price after deducting transportation cost.[11] When gold was a necessary part of financial activities, the cost of shipping gold between geographic areas is a part of interest costs.

Information costs are another explanation for variations in the interest rate between regions. Certainly this could account for differences in interest rates in different locations around the turn of the century, when telegraphs were expensive and telephones still a novelty.

A bank might be offering a product at a lower price but customers of other banks might not be aware of this. Or a firm may not compete where it could be successful because it is unfamiliar with the market. The potential borrower will shop for a loan only until the additional cost of further shopping offsets the expected savings in cost. As George Stigler says "there is no 'imperfection' in a market possessing incomplete knowledge if it would not be remunerative to acquire complete knowledge."[12] As rural borrowers will incur expense when applying to city banks for a loan, they will frequently settle for a more expensive local loan. The firm close to the market can charge a price slightly above the level other banks would charge because it knows other firms must incur costs to enter the market. Information costs then provide some protection from competition for the local firm.

The function of a market is to facilitate exchange. If transaction costs are assumed away, the efficient market will achieve every desired exchange of homogeneous goods at a single price. There must be only one price; otherwise some seller would be receiving less than some other buyer is paying and both would prefer to trade with one another than with whomever they are trading.[13] Even if the market were efficient, the reality of imperfect knowledge would cause variations in interest rates. These variations should just compensate for differences in risk or cost. Any variation above this will attract new firms into the higher priced market. That is, new banks will open in the area, old banks will start branches, or banks outside the area will increase their loans to the area.

The conditions under which a market will be presumed to be efficient differ depending on the writer. It is generally conceded that a perfectly competitive model is appropriately used in situations where there are a large number of sellers with a homogeneous product, and there are no barriers to entry to the market. Because of the limited amount of government regulation, the capital market in California would seem to meet this requirement.

Over the period being analyzed in this paper, California experienced a maturing of the economy. The rapid growth of population after the discovery of gold had declined and the state was developing a more diverse economy. New areas were settled, and some gold and silver towns were abandoned. The railroad linked the urban areas, roads were built, and communications improved. The financial market may not have been perfectly integrated before or after the period studied, but it should have improved over this time. Economic historians have noted the existence of interest rate differentials between regions and the decline that occurs in these as economic development proceeds. Rondo Cameron is one of these historians. He notes "improvement of financial markets should...produce a narrowing of the dispersion of interest rates among different types of users, among geographic regions, and over periods of seasonal fluctuation."[14]

METHODS OF TESTING FOR MONOPOLY POWER

There is a large body of literature related to the measurement of overall monopoly power. As yet, no simple measure has been discovered. The most frequently used index of market power is the concentration ratio. This is simply the share of the total of some economic variable (employment, sales, assets, etc.) for all firms in a market accounted for by a relatively few of the largest firms in that market. In contemporary studies of banking concentration the usual concentration ratio is the share of total bank deposits or assets held by the three largest banks in the local market.[15] But the selection of the number of banks is arbitrary and the ratio is not sensitive to all aspects of market power. The number of banks and the size disparity between the largest banks and other banks can change without affecting the ratio. The Herfindahl index is a variation on the concentration ratio which is often used in banking. This index is the sum of the squared market share of each firm.[16] In banking studies the Herfindahl technique has been used with shares of deposits and assets, but there are also problems with this index. A smaller inequality in bank size in a market can be offset by a smaller number of banks. When the number of banks tends to be small in most of the markets being compared, the problem is severe. This may account for the limited use of Herfindahl and other concentration measures in historical studies of banking. Historical studies have generally used the number of banks in the market as the best measure of monopoly power.[17]

Instead of attempting to measure concentration directly and incurring these difficulties, many researchers instead attempt to discern the effects of monopoly. In areas where concentration is greater, interest rates should be higher and this fact has been used as the basis for monopoly tests. If the monopolist is not able to perfectly discriminate, the output should also be lower relative to more competitive areas. In early historical studies, the direct use of interest rates is rare, since information on interest rates is scarce.[18]

Lance Davis was the first to attempt to reconstruct a proxy for past interest rates. This allowed him to use the price difference test for variation in monopoly power between regions. He reasoned that gross earnings should represent the interest received from loans or securities hold by the bank. He excluded bank building and fixtures and funds due from other banks from assets. The ratio of gross earnings to the remaining assets should approximate the interest rate paid by borrowers.[19] This technique was also used by Sylla in his 1965 study. Gene Smiley used a variation of the Davis proxy which included the funds due from other bankers, contending that these correspondent deposits usually paid interest. Margaret Myers reported this interest on correspondent deposits ranged from three to six percent in New York. John James claimed, however, that this rate had dropped and stabilized at two percent by 1880, and ranged from two and one half to three percent outside of New York.[20] Smiley excluded government bonds from assets on the basis of their probable use as backing for note issue.

While the Davis proxy from interest rates has been used frequently in other studies, it does require data on gross earnings of banks and some detail about their assets. This information is generally inaccessible for state banks, which form the majority of banks in the period. It is also unavailable for national banks in the years before 1888. Davis used the ratio of net earnings to earning assets as a proxy for interest rates in these years. It is undoubtedly an inferior proxy especially for large regions because operating expenses and taxes were likely to vary between different areas. James pointed out that taxes were a relatively large part of the difference between net and gross earnings and were based on capital and note circulation.[21] Therefore larger banks, more likely to have monopoly power, had higher taxes.

Their net earnings might show little variation from those of smaller banks which did not have monopoly power. When the banks earned premiums on government bonds they could be charged against earnings. These charges were arbitrary as to timing and would also reduce the usefulness of net earnings to assets as a proxy for interest rates.[22] James illustrated this by showing the low correlation between net earnings and gross earnings for the years when both are available.[23]

In some cases, even net earnings data are not available. Davis found little information on savings and loan companies or other sources of long term loans included in the reports on national banks. To form an estimate of long term interest rate differentials, he developed a proxy for interest rates that can be constructed with only the information available on balance statements. Bankers, given two equal risk investment opportunities, will select more of that which has the highest (expected) return. Also, the securities market is broader than the loan market available to any one bank. Therefore a bank in a high-interest area will tend to put a larger portion of its assets in loans rather than into securities. Using this reasoning, Davis justified an interest rate proxy consisting of the ratio of loans to loans plus securities.[24]

It would also be possible to support the theory that market power exists by proving that capital could not move freely into areas where it is scarce, Conversely, proof that capital could move freely would make it difficult for exceedingly high interest rates to exist in one area. Any difference in interest rates observed in this situation would probably be due to differences in risk or cost of lending.

TESTING CALIFORNIA FOR EFFICIENT MARKETS

In the current study, all of these tests will be used in some form to reveal information about the financial structure in California. It is possible to derive concentration ratios of the several types mentioned. Information is accessible on deposits and assets of the individual banks, savings banks, trust companies and private banks in the state. However, some preliminary work by Roger Lister indicated this may not be a fruitful task. Many counties had only one bank, so normal techniques of selecting the top three banks in a market would be unreasonable. Using the percentage of assets or deposit held by the one largest bank would produce highly unsatisfactory indicators of concentration. Lister uses Herfindahl indexes for deposits, loans and assets. His indexes did not show great variation between the three market share indicators, and he used the number of banks in a market as an alternate concentration measure.[25] This study examines only the number of banks in a market.

There are some data available on interest rates. Banks reported average interest received per month on loans in 1879, in their first year of reporting to the state board of bank commissioners. Limited tests for differences in the mean interest rates are made on this material.

Commercial banks in 1879 also reported the interest paid on deposits, and savings banks provided this information for every year after 1879. If differences in these interest rates occur between markets, it may indicate that depositors do not search for the bank paying highest interest rates. The local bank or banks must have some monopoly power to keep their depositors while paying interest lower than that which could be received elsewhere. While these variations in interest do not necessarily indicate differences in the price of loans, they would support the thesis of an imperfect capital market. Furthermore, in locations where the interest on loans is higher, banks would have the incentive to pay higher interest on deposits to attract additional funds for lending.

Gross earnings and the balance statements of individual banks are available for the California savings banks for the years after 1880, making it possible to replicate the interest rate proxy developed by Davis and modified by Smiley and James. Similar numbers are not available for commercial banks. In 1879, gross earnings were not available for any type of financial institution. Net earnings were reported for commercial and savings banks individually this year. Balance statements were not presented in a manner which allows the separation of earning assets, so the proxy for 1879 is necessarily net earnings divided by total assets.

As Davis noted, the proxy using only balance statement information is the least reliable. Smiley and James attack this aspect of the Davis research heavily.[26] It obviously should only be used where better information is unavailable. Although the detailed information on California banks is difficult to gain access to, the effort may yield better results. The measure of the ratio of loans to loans plus securities is left to other researchers.[27]

An attempt was made to locate and provide evidence of capital mobility. Testing the Sylla hypothesis requires information regarding the flow of capital between rural and urban banks in order to determine whether country banks actually deposited funds in city banks to earn interest. It is also important to prove the markets were sufficiently separated for price discrimination to occur. Evidence that city banks lent to rural borrowers would not support the hypothesized rural bankers' ability to charge high and discriminatory interest rates to their local borrowers.

DEFINING THE MARKET AND PRODUCT

Any indicator of concentration requires defining the relevant product and the market areas for these products. The standard metropolitan statistical area is used for most studies of the modern banking industrial structure, simply because the data are available. It may be that the appropriate market area is the metropolitan area. Smaller customers of a bank, households and small businesses, because of traditional banking practice and convenience, rely heavily on banks within a few miles. But it might be more appropriate to use a much larger area. Using a larger area, however, risks underestimates of concentration.

Historical studies have also tended toward defining the market by the available data. Davis' source for information was the annual reports of the Comptroller of the Currency. The Comptroller aggregated all reported earnings by state or reserve city. It is most easily available in the summaries which group the results into five regions and reserve cities. Davis then defines the relevant market as the comptroller's regions. This definition of the market was followed by the later researchers of the late nineteenth century United States, although Smiley and James make some modifications in the regions.

It would be difficult to define the appropriate market for nineteenth century California banking. The product was probably not designed for the small business or household consumer. Most historical work indicates banks primarily served large commercial customers. This can be verified by data on the size of loans or deposit accounts. For the present, it seems best to follow tradition and define the market according to the available data.

Most census data and property tax information was reported by county, and banks reported the loans on real estate by county. Therefore the county is used as the market area. For many tests the counties are grouped into regions. With small amounts and uncertain reliability of data, the grouping was used to increase accuracy. There were often many counties where no reports were available, or the particular information needed was reported by few banks. This problem is also solved by grouping the counties into regions.

Even where the data is reported by region, the market definition will certainly be more accurate than the much larger regions of the United States used by Davis and others. Only Richard Keehn made an earlier attempt to identify markets within a state.[28]

Other studies necessarily ignored the competition national commercial banks face from state banks and other types of financial institutions. In most states the national banks had close competition from state-chartered banks, but the lack of available data on state banks forced their exclusion from the studies. It is intended that this, and similar studies, will remedy this gap in knowledge. Only a systematic, state-by-state effort will yield the information necessary to construct an accurate portrayal of the United States financial structure.

For this study state banks are emphasized. In California, the state banks provided most of the banking services in the nineteenth century. National banks were not common until after 1900. Concentration on national banks is not likely to lead to accurate results in this or other states where the situation was similar.

Most of the products and services offered by commercial banks in the nineteenth century were also offered by other financial institutions.[29] It is probable competition from savings banks and associations, home savings groups, private bankers, and other groups has been ignored because of the difficulty of obtaining data. However, their exclusion has undoubtedly led to mistakes in assessing the extent of competition. Therefore, this study includes those financial institutions which would be likely to compete with commercial banks.

In California, savings banks constituted such close competition for commercial banks that, in many cases, it is impossible to distinguish between the two. Both offered the same products and services.[30] Therefore, savings banks are included in all tests. Trust companies are included for the same reason. Where possible, the activities of private bankers are also taken into account.

This study also includes the activities of "banks in liquidation." The California State Board of Bank Commissioners reports several times that banks sometimes used the liquidation procedure as a technique for avoiding unpleasant obligations (to depositors, for example), while still operating. The board complained that some liquidating banks conducted their business, often without any change in management for excessive periods of time.[31] Building and loan associations were active in California in the nineteenth century, and reports on their activities are available for the years after 1893. Because of the lack of data for the earlier years covered in this study, the activities of these organizations were not included.[32] Life insurance companies may have competed in the loan market but due to the lack of data were also not included.

The basic technique used in this study is to desegregate California into different markets and test for statistically significant differences between markets. As mentioned, the county was the most basic market unit. There were from forty-two to fifty-seven counties in California during the period. When these were grouped by region, the first attempt was to keep counties with similar economies in the same region. The first grouping identified counties as urban, agricultural, or mining economies. However, the counties identified as mining counties contained too few banks to generate useful comparison with other regions. The agricultural and mining categories were merged into "rural." As the basic nature of the economies of the counties seem to depend primarily on geographic location, the rural category was subdivided into northern, central, and southern. The counties in the northern rural category were primarily engaged in mining, timber, cattle ranching and the cultivation of nuts and fruits. These counties experienced declines in the mining related areas over the period.[33] The counties in the central rural region engaged primarily in land intensive agriculture. During the period under consideration, the main crop was wheat.[34] The southern rural counties experienced the most change in their economies over the period. In 1878, these counties were very much undeveloped. Large areas were devoted to the cultivation of range cattle and there were scattered agriculturally oriented settlements. In the 1880's the world discovered the area's pleasant climate and the tourist industry brought economic development.[35] The character of the region changed rapidly after that. The cattle ranges were broken up by sheep ranches and citrus groves. Increasing use of irrigation allowed the cultivation of a wide variety of crops. And the population grew rapidly.

San Francisco is used as the sole urban county for earlier years of study. Los Angeles is separated from the southern rural region and added to San Francisco for comparisons using data from later years. Because an exact dating of when Los Angeles became "urban" would be arbitrary, comparisons are made with both definitions of urban in tests involving 1889 and 1894 data. It should be noted that in cases when banks are placed into regions by location, only banks located in the city of Los Angeles are classified as urban. Other Los Angeles county banks are left in the "southern rural" category unless otherwise noted. For certain tests there are variations from the grouping pattern described above. The variations will be discussed in later sections.

The technique used to test for significant differences between the markets involves computing the mean value of some statistic for each market. The difference in these mean values are tested for statistical significance by computing the t-value for differences in means (non-paired values).[36] The specific technique used for each test will be described in detail in later sessions.

DATA ON CALIFORNIA BANKING HISTORY

Once the theoretical base is determined, the appropriate market selected, and the group of potential competitors defined, the implementation of the tests awaits the availability of data. As in most historical studies, this stage has created the greatest difficulty. Most studies have worked with the most accessible data, that from the reports of the Comptroller of the Currency. However, the first of these studies occurred more than a decade ago and it is unlikely that improvements can occur in the portrayal of nineteenth century United States banking history without the infusion of new data. As mentioned above, the most severe problem with the data used in other studies is the exclusion of state-chartered banks and of financial institutions other than commercial banks. Therefore, the most potential for improvement in the accuracy of these studies would come from increased accessibility to national banks. As each state had different legal restrictions and market factors to consider, this data collection task is best undertaken individually for each state. Richard Keehn pioneered the effort with his studies of Wisconsin, and this study continues the effort by making available information on banking in California.[37]

When the California legislature passed the Banking Act of 1878, they became one of few states requiring banks to publish information about their financial condition. The Comptroller reports on national banks, which commenced in 1873, abstracted earnings and dividends for the national banks by state, territory or reserve city. The Comptroller's reports also contained the balance statements of national banks. It is possible these reports might have inspired the desire of the California legislature to acquire information about the banks within the state, none of which were national banking system members at that time.

The first report of the newly created California Board of Bank Commissioners was dated June 30, 1878. The commissioners may have used some information from an article in the *Evening Bulletin*, February 22, 1878. This article presented information alleged to be from the semi-annual statements of California banks for December 31, 1877.[38] At first, two reports were issued from the Board of Bank Commisssioners, one to the governor of the state, and one to the legislature. The report to the governor was generally a very brief comment on the state of the banking industry. The report to the legislature was more complete. The dates on these reports do not coincide. After 1880, both reports were published together, and volumes usually contained both of the semi-annual reports made during each calendar year. The dates on the reports do not remain entirely consistent, but they usually were presented to the legislature June 30 or July 1, and to the governor on January 1.

Apparently the reports received little attention from either the governor or the legislature, since the board frequently used its reports to complain of the fruitlessness of their efforts. The report to the governor August 10, 1880 contained a typical comment:

> The Board has been in existence for nine years...over and over it has pointed out the necessity for legislation...yet, so far, not the least notice has been taken of their reports, or of any suggestion made in those reports.[39]

The lack of interest in these reports resulted in some inconsistencies that make them less useful to researchers. The state legislature neglected to provide the funds to publish the reports in 1881, 1892, 1898, 1901, 1902, 1903 and 1904.[40] Except for these years, the reports were made semi-annually from 1878 to 1894. After that date, they were published annually. The data provided in most reports is similar. The Board commented on new banks, name changes and mergers. In early years they provided the names of banks retiring from business as well. Some data aggregated by San Francisco or all rural banks is supplied, which is compiled from balance statements of individual banks. Comparison of major assets and liabilities is made with previous years.

A great deal of information on individual banks is provided in the appendix to the reports to the legislature (see Table 22, appendix for a complete description of the information provided). Until 1909, banks were separated into savings banks and commercial banks. The classification was made only according to whether they were formed under the savings bank act of 1862, or under the state's general incorporation laws, not according to the nature of their business. The reports required from the two groups differed, especially after the first few years (see Table 23, appendix). Reports from private bankers were requested in 1878, and after, but few complied until they were required to do so in 1886.[41] Reports were also provided for "banks in liquidation" every year.

The bank commissioner examined every bank under their jurisdiction twice annually in earlier years and at least once every year until 1905. Their revision of each bank's balance statement was published in the appendix of the report to the legislature. The commissioners wrote off bad debts and often reduced the value of real estate carried on the books.

For most years the banks' reports on assets and liabilities were summarized in tabular form at the end of each report. This makes them considerably more accessible than the revised statement of the bank commissioners. The use of these reports, however, will bias results, and it should be noted that the accuracy of the data may have suffered from banks' attempts at "window dressing."

As one of the major tasks undertaken by this study was the collection and presentation of the data contained in the reports of the bank commissioners, some notice should be made of the other problems encountered in the process. When it became obvious that missing years would cause problems in time series analysis and that more detailed information would be illuminating, it was decided to emphasize key years. The dates most closely corresponding to the population census dates were judged as having the most interest to economic historians. Years midway between each of the census years were added to increase the number of data points. Most generalizations were drawn from all six years: 1879 (real estate data was from July 1878, as it was not collected in 1879), 1884, 1889, 1894, 1899, and 1905 (as 1904 remains unpublished). Some analysis emphasized differences in behavior between financial institutions. Where this cross-sectional analysis was appropriate, the years 1879, 1889 and 1899 were used where possible. Often 1879 data were excluded because of the small number of banks reporting.

Grouping by county created some difficulty in counties which changed their boundaries over the period. Five counties were created during this time from sections of other counties. Orange County was established in 1889 from the southern part of Los Angeles County. Glenn County was established in 1891 from the southern half of Colusa County. A general reorganization took place in 1893, making part of Fresno County into Madera, part of Tulare County into King County, and creating Riverside County from the southern part of San Bernardino County and a northeastern section of San Diego County. The Imperial Valley had minor economic significance throughout all but the last few years covered by this study and did not separate from San Diego County until 1909, so its existence was not made explicit. Whenever possible, a bank was listed located in the county of jurisdiction for 1905. For example, a bank located in Monroeville was always listed as in Glenn County, even though Glenn County was not created until 1891. In the case of reported loans on real estate, the bank cited the location of the real estate by county only. As a result, it was impossible to identify the exact location of the land. For the tests involving the real estate reports, the contemporary boundaries were used.

NOTES

1. Edwin Mansfield, *Microeconomics: Theory and Applications*, Shorter second ed. (New York: W.W. Norton & Co., 1976) pp. 229-230. George Stigler, *The Theory of Prices*, 3rd ed. (New York: Macmillan Co., 1966), pp. 210-213.

2. Lester Chandler, *The Economics of Money and Banking,* 6th ed. (New York: Harper and Row Publishers, 1973), p. 69.

3. Richard F. Wacht, "Branch Banking and Risk," *Journal of Financial and Quantitative Analysis* 3 (March 1968), p. 106. Also Ernst Baltensperger, "Economics of Scale, Firm Size and Concentration in Banking," *Journal of Money, Credit, and Banking* 4 (August 1972), p. 467.

4. Basil J. Moors, *An Introduction to the Theory of Finance: Assetholder Behavior Under Uncertainty.* (New York: The Free Press, 1968), pp. 98-100.

5. *Ibid.*, pp. 467-468, discusses the possibility that one source of scale economies is uncertainty. A larger number of deposits means more stable deposit-volume and less excess reserves. A bank holds a capital account to protect against losses and the related risk of insolvency. Losses expected form a probability distribution. Increasing the number of assets will reduce the variance of this distribution and allow reduction of the capital to asset ratio.

6. George Stigler, "The Division of Labor is Limited to the Extent of the Market," *Journal of Political Economy* 59 (June 1951), pp. 185-193.

7. George E. Barnett, *State Banking and Trust Companies Since the Passing of the National Banking Act* 61st Congress 3rd session, document no. 659 (Washington, D.C., G.P.O. 1911), provides the details of these restrictions.

8. See George Stigler, "Perfect Competition Historically Contemplated" in *Essays in the History of Economics* (Chicago: University of Chicago Press, 1965), pp. 234-267, for a complete discussion of various definitions of competition.

9. John A. James, "Banking Market Structure, Risk and the Pattern of Local Interest Rates in the US, 1893-1911" *Review of Economics and Statistics* 58 (November, 1976), pp. 453-462.

10. Most of the modern financial literature explicitly includes some type of premium for risk, and the theory for determining the size of that premium is fairly well defined. Much of this work has depended on the contributions of William Sharpe. See particularly "Capital Asset Prices: A Theory of Market Equilibrium Under Conditions of Risk," *Journal of Finance* 19 (September, 1964), pp. 425-42. Some tests for monopolies in nineteenth century US banking have attempted to explicitly allow for the risk premium. James and Rockoff regularly incorporate a variable for past losses when predicting bank behavior.

11. *Ibid.*, Stigler refers to information costs as "the costs of transportation from ignorance to omniscience," p. 291.

12. Stigler, "Perfect Competition, Historically Contemplated," discusses previous definition.

13. George Stigler, "Imperfections in the Capital Market," *Journal of Political Economy* 75, (June, 1967), pp. 287-293.

14. Rondo Cameron, quoted in, Richard Keehn, "Federal Bank Policy, Bank Market Structure and Bank Performance: Wisconsin, 1863-1914," *Business History Review* 48 (Spring, 1971), p. 15.

15. Paul Smith, "Measures of Banking Structure and Competition," *Federal Reserve Bulletin* 51 (September, 1965), pp. 1212-1222.

16. The Herfindahl index was developed by Orris C. Herfindahl for his Ph.D. dissertation, *Concentration on the Steel Industry* (New York: Columbia University Press, 1950).

17. Roger Lister, "Market Structure and Economic Performance: California Banking, 1896-1900," paper presented at Western Economic Association meetings, Anaheim, California, June 1977, used several variations in concentration ratios, and the Herfindahl index, and concluded that the number of banks is a superior measure of concentration. Richard Keehn, "Federal Bank Policy, Bank Market Structure and Bank Performance, Wisconsin, 1863-1914," also uses the number of banks as the best measure of concentration.

18. Not withstanding Sidney Homer's *A History of Interest Rates: 200 B.C. to the Present* (New Brunswick, New Jersey, 1963).

19. Lance Davis, "The Investment Market, 1870-1914: The Evolution of a National Market," *Journal of Economic History* 25 (September 1965), p.357.

20. Margaret Myers, *The New York Money Market, Origins and Development.* (New York: Columbia University Press, 1931), p. 122. John James, "A Note on Interest Paid on New York Bankers' Balances in the Postbellum Period," *Business History Review* 50 (Summer 1976), p. 200.

21. John James, "Banking Market Structure," p. 445.

22. *Ibid.*, p. 453.

23. *Ibid.*, p. 454.

24. Davis, p. 378.

25. Lister, p. 15.

26. Davis, p. 378; Gene Smiley, "Interest Rate Movements in the United States, 1888-1913," *Journal of Economic History* 35 (September 1973), pp. 594-595: James, "Banking Market Structure," p. 454.

27. Lister, used this measure for his 1977 paper. In his book, *Bank Behavior and Regulation, and Economic Development: California 1860-1910* (New York: Garland Publishing, 1993), Lister uses loan to asset

ratios as the dependent variable predicted by the age of the bank, size, and risk adversion.

28. Richard H. Keehn, "Federal Bank Policy, Bank Market Structure and Bank Performance: Wisconsin 1863-1914," *Business History Review* 48 (Spring 1974), p. 1-27.

29. Bray Hammond, *Banks and Politics in America from the Revolution to the Civil War* (Princeton: Princeton University Press, 1957), describes a variety of early alternatives to commercial banks.

30. Leroy Armstrong and J.O. Denny, *Financial California: An Historical Review of the Beginning and Progress of Banking in the State* (San Francisco: The Coast Banker Publishing Co., 1916), p. 167.

31. Board of Bank Commissioners, Report 1885: "The Commission requests (again) passage of a law to compel insolvent banks to close business in a reasonable length of time, because banks are liquidating slowly after ceasing to pay depositors."

32. Building and Loan Association Commissioners, *Annual Report*, 1893/94 to 1903/4; 1893-94, 1894/95 and 1895/96 are printed in the appendices to California Legislature Jols. 31 session Vol. 4 (unnumbered document), jls 32 session vol. 7 (Doc.1 and 2). 1896/97 and 1897/98 were not printed.

33. Edward V. Salitore, *California Information Almanac: Past, Present, Future* (Lakewood, CA.: Edward V. Salitore, 1973), p. 535-570.

34. John J, Powell, *The Golden State and Its Resources*, (San Francisco: Bacon and Co., 1874).

35. Glenn S. Dunke, *The Boom of the Eighties in Southern California* (San Marino, CA.: Huntington Library, 1966. Originally published 1944).

36. The formula can be found in any beginning statistics book. See for example: Joseph G. Monks and Byron L. Newton, *Statistics for Business,* (Science Research Associates, Inc., 1988).

37. See also, Roger Lister, *Bank Behavior, Regulation, and Economic Development: California, 1860-1910.*

38. Actually the legislature passed a law in the fall of 1875 that, effective in 1876, every banker must publish semi-annual statements of certain resources and liabilities in newspapers in their area (Armstrong and Denny, p. 22), but there was no penalty for non-compliance and no records exist of these statements. Benjamin Wright, in *Banking in California, 1849-1910,* p. 73, claims that he compiled the balance statements for the February 22 issue of the Evening Bulletin and that the figures published there were used by the Board to determine the initial licensing fees for banks in existence in 1878.

39. Board of Bank Commissioners, *Report to the Governor*, August 10, 1886.

40. The 1905 report of the Board contains the reports to the governor for 1901, 1902, 1903, 1904 with a comment on the legislature's failure to provide the funds for printing those or the more comprehensive reports to the legislature. A similar comment appears in the 1899 report concerning 1897 and 1898. No records can be found concerning the fate of the 1881 and 1892 reports or the material collected for the unpublished later reports. Ira Cross seems to have had access to this material for his *Financing and Empire: The History of Banking in California* (San Francisco: S.J. Clarke Publishing Co., 1927).

41. Benjamin Wright, *Banking in California, 1849-1910.* (San Francisco: H.S. Crocker Company, 1910), p. 85.

IV

EVIDENCE ON INTEREST RATE DIFFERENTIALS

INTEREST RATE TESTS

Since the interest rates are prices for funds loaned by banks, the most direct test of the hypothesis that local monopolies characterized the financial markets of California would be a test of variation in interest rates between areas. This test has long been hampered by the lack of data on interest rate levels. Sylla, Davis and others have tested for interest rate differentials by using a proxy for interest rates, the ratio of earnings to earnings assets.[1] Even this test has been impeded considerably by a lack of data. Net earnings by geographic area are fairly accessible for national banks, but most appropriate gross earnings figures are not available for state or even early national banks.

The problem of insufficient information is also relevant to California state banks. There is only one year in which interest rates on loans are recorded at all. In 1879, commercial banks reported average monthly interest rates charged on loans. Thirty-nine banks reported this information, and the interest rates range from .88 percent to 1.5 percent per month. Only one San Francisco bank reports; their interest is 1.0 percent per month. Northern banks had interest charges averaging 1.24 percent over ten banks reporting. Eighteen banks outside San Francisco in the central part of the state reported an average rate of 1.08 percent and the eight southern banks averaged a rate of 1.34 percent (see table 24, appendix). Observation indicates substantial differences between the areas of California, and seem to support the idea that San Francisco was an important, competitive financial center. The concept of local monopolies does not seem to be supported by variations in interest rates between counties. For instance, in the southern area where wide open space segregated lenders, five of the eight lenders charged 1.5 percent average monthly interest. The mode in northern counties was 1.25 percent.[2]

It is unfortunate that the bank commissioners did not continue to request information on interest charged. They did, however, request reports on the interest or dividends paid to depositors at the bank.

Commercial banks and savings banks continued to report on interest paid until 1909.

If the interest rate paid depositors varies significantly between different areas, it could be said the hypothesis is supported. The significant differences in interest rates allowed by monopoly power do exist. This, however, is certainly not conclusive proof. First, the sample is neither representative nor random, as it is limited to savings banks (after 1879). This is a weak criticism, as savings banks differed little from commercial banks. They offered term and ordinary demand accounts and competed in the loan markets with commercial banks, although savings banks did have a larger portion of their loans in real estate.[3] Second, the differences that show up might be due to differences in risk or information cost in different areas.

A bank in an area where interest on loans is high would have reason to pay high rates to its depositors. If opportunities for capital investment are profitable enough to allow the payment of high interest rates on loans, financial institutions should have to pay higher interest rates to successfully attract deposits.[4] When simple correlation tests were run between interest paid depositors and interest received on loans, the correlation was not extremely high. The R^2 for interest paid on term accounts and interest received on loans is 0.4769 over thirty-two banks, and the R^2 for ordinary accounts is 0.5157 for seventeen banks. Certainly, the variation in interest rates paid on deposits by banks does not fully explain variation in interest received on loans.

Much variation in interest received will be due to the wide variety of loans made by the banks in different areas. The range of interest received must have been very wide when the loans made by banks were secured by everything from wolf pelts, through crops in the field and school bonds, to government securities. The average interest rate received would probably be rather unstable, and not compare well with the interest paid on deposits.

Since we have only one set of interest rates banks charged on loans, extensive examination would not lead to useful generalization. Because of this, we turn to interest paid on deposits. Interest rates could vary significantly between counties primarily characterized by different industries because of differences in risk. Therefore, there was an attempt to group counties by industry. The primary industries were agriculture, mining, and such other activities that could be comfortable characterized as "urban" in nature. The mining industry caused some difficulty. There were some banks which could be classified as mining banks. However, they are always too few to form a separate group. There also are some areas where mining and farming co-existed and made separation difficult. Because of these difficulties, the final classification became urban/rural activities.

Table 1 summarizes the results of comparisons of mean interest paid to depositors between regions. When interest rates paid by savings banks in rural counties are compared for northern California versus central California, t-value tests do not reveal differences significant at the ninety percent level in ordinary interest rates for any of the six years tested. The interest rate comparisons for term deposits show a difference in only one comparison, 1879.

TABLE 1

DIFFERENCES IN MEAN INTEREST RATE
PAID ON DEPOSITS

Term

Test	1879	1884	1889	1894	1898	1905
Between Rural Areas:						
north vs. central	*	-	-	0	0	0
north vs. south	0	-	-	0	**	**
south vs. central	0	-	0	0	0	**
S.F. vs. rural north	**	***	-	0	0	0
S.F. vs. rural south	**	-	0	0	***	0
S.F. vs. rural central	***	0	0	0	*	0
urban vs. rural	**	0	0	0	0	*
S.F. Bay area vs. other counties	***	*	*	0	0	*
other counties vs. S.F.	**	0	0	0	**	0

-	insufficient data
0	difference not significant
*	difference significant at ninety percent level of confidence
**	difference siginificant at ninety five percent level of confidence
***	difference significant at ninety nine percent level of confidence

Further detail is provided in the appendix, tables 25-33.

TABLE 1 (CONTINUED)

DIFFERENCES IN MEAN INTEREST RATE PAID ON DEPOSITS

Ordinary

Test	1879	1884	1889	1894	1898	1905
Between Rural Areas:						
north vs. central	0	0	0	0	0	0
north vs. south	0	-	0	***	***	**
south vs. central	0	-	0	***	***	0
S.F. vs. rural north	0	*	*	*	0	0
S.F. vs. rural south	***	-	0	**	***	0
S.F. vs. rural central	0	***	0	0	**	0
urban vs. rural	*	**	*	0	0	0
S.F. Bay area vs. other counties	***	**	0	***	0	0
other counties vs. S.F.	*	***	0	0	0	0

-	insufficient data
0	difference not significant
*	difference significant at ninety percent level of confidence
**	difference siginificant at ninety five percent level of confidence
***	difference significant at ninety nine percent level of confidence

Further detail is provided in the appendix, tables 25-33.

When northern California savings banks are compared with southern California banks, with central California excluded, differences significant at the ninety percent level occur in later years, but not in earlier years. Differences are highly significant for ordinary interest rates in 1894 and 1898, and fairly significant for term interest in 1898 and 1905. As Table 2 shows, the average interest rates paid on deposits produces a curious pattern. The northern counties have higher interest rates in 1894, but in 1898 and 1905, ordinary interest rates are higher in northern California and term interest rates are lower. One possible explanation is that the active real estate market in southern California during the 1890's provided strong attraction for long term funds and the smoothing differences on interest rates was not complete.

Comparing interest rates for southern and central counties, excluding San Francisco, highly significant differences show up in 1894 and 1898, but only in ordinary interest rates. The ordinary rate is much higher in central California. It is quite likely then, that the phenomenal growth of southern California during this period distorted interest rates temporarily. It would be informative to determine whether the situation had changed by the time the southern area had survived its first land boom, but there is no information on interest rates paid on deposits after 1906.

TABLE 2

INTEREST RATE PAID ON DEPOSITS

Ordinary

Area	1879	1884	1889	1894	1898	1905
North	6.375	4.125	5.000	4.157	3.540	3.143
Central	6.786	4.550	4.575	4.474	3.972	3.215
South	7.833	-	3.750	3.300	3.045	3.135
All Banks	6.711	3.794	4.222	4.031	3.569	3.175
S.F. Banks	6.175	6.483	4.137	4.211	3.418	3.237
All other Banks	7.212	4.337	4.319	4.009	3.609	3.164
Rural Banks	6.977	4.350	4.633	4.150	3.674	3.203
Urban Banks	6.293	3.585	3.998	3.848	3.477	3.146
Bay Area	6.172	3.585	4.143	4.386	3.710	3.188

Term

Area	1879	1884	1889	1894	1898	1905
North	8.638	5.000	-	5.129	3.875	3.300
Central	7.910	4.467	4.810	5.103	4.360	3.692
South	8.422	-	5.333	4.967	4.442	4.021
All Banks	8.015	4.425	4.855	5.055	4.278	3.888
S.F. Banks	7.261	4.260	4.714	5.032	3.956	3.550
All other Banks	8.254	4.543	4.931	4.060	4.363	3.901
Rural Banks	8.211	4.583	4.956	5.080	4.291	3.759
Urban Banks	7.468	4.267	4.773	5.014	4.267	4.003
Bay Area	7.426	4.229	4.664	5.086	4.089	3.586

Further details are provided in table 34 in the appendix.

When comparisons between regions were made, no significant trends appear which support the hypothesis of local monopoly. There is evidence of a sluggish response in capital movement to the rapid growth of southern California on the land boom of the 1890's, but this certainly does not conflict with accepted free market theory.

Sylla would not find it surprising that, when only rural areas are compared, more differences do not appear. He theorized that rural bankers all could price discriminate in their own market. The rate city banks would pay for their deposits provided a floor, so rural interest rates should be higher than the rates city banks pay on deposits, but they would not necessarily differ from each other.[5]

It would be informative then to compare the interest rates by rural banks with those paid by city banks. San Francisco is the only definite financial center in this period, although the number of banks in Los Angeles county begins to rise rapidly by 1890 and matches the number in San Francisco by 1889. In 1905, there are twenty-nine banks in San Francisco County and fifty-one in Los Angeles County, although only nineteen of these were located in the city of Los Angeles. Pasadena and the port region each contributed about ten to the balance and other Los Angeles County cities made up the total. There were other cities in the state with more than a scattered few banks. The bay area always had large numbers of banks compared to other counties. Riverside and San Diego possessed a surprising number of banks in 1899 and 1905 (see table 23, appendix).

The first tests use San Francisco as the urban financial center. San Francisco borrowers generally paid lower interest rates than other counties (see table 2), but the difference is significant at the ninety percent level for both rates only in 1879, on ordinary rates in 1884, and in term rates in 1898. Only 1884 differs at the ninety-nine percent level of significance (see table 1). San Francisco was then compared separately with each rural area. When San Francisco was compared with northern California, scattered differences of significance occur. Northern counties generally charged higher interest than San Francisco. The difference is great for term interest rates in 1879 and 1884 and barely significant for ordinary rates in 1884, 1889 and 1894. Comparing San Francisco with the South again reveals the aberrations of the 1890s decade. Ordinary interest rates in 1894 and 1898 are higher than in southern California, term interest rates are lower, and the differences are significant at the ninety-nine percent level.

The most interesting test is to compare San Francisco with

nearby rural areas. If differences appear here, it is less likely they are due to high information and transaction cost associated with great, and in this period, arduous distance. Generally, agricultural central California banks usually appear to pay higher interest rates than San Francisco banks, but the difference is not often significant. As table 1 shows, there were differences in term interest rates in 1879, and ordinary rates have a highly significant difference in 1884, although the sample was small. Significant differences are also apparent in 1898, but eight of the twelve comparisons in the six year sample show no significant difference.

Again, the only strong result is that term rates were unusually high in southern California. In other comparisons, significant differences show up less often in later years of the sample. Although the results are rather weak, they do not refute the hypothesis that the capital market is improving over time, and might even be said to give weak support to the hypothesis. The urban versus rural area comparison particularly supports the Davis theory of declining differences in interest rates.

As previously mentioned, other definitions of urban areas are possible. Oakland appears to have had an active financial center, and Los Angeles certainly was important after 1890. When San Francisco, Alameda and Los Angeles are combined and compared with all other counties, we find they almost always had lower interest rates. The differences are significant for all interest rates paid in 1879 and for ordinary rates in 1884 and 1889. A difference also appears in term rates in 1905, although the level of significance on the differences never exceeds ninety-five percent and rarely is above ninety percent. In years when support for this definition of urban areas exists, evidence does not support the existence of differences between these urban areas and other areas.

The active San Francisco area apparently bred high levels of financial activity in Oakland and Berkeley and also in less-urban areas. San Jose, Santa Cruz and even Gilroy, Dixon, and Martinez seem to have had more than their share of banks (table 23, appendix). To test the possibility that this fringe area was smoothing differences between San Francisco and other areas, comparison was made between the counties bordering San Francisco Bay and other areas. About half of the comparisons show differences are most significant and consistent for 1879 and 1884.

These comparisons do not provide convincing support for the

hypothesis that rural bankers held monopoly positions and charged higher average interest rates because of their ability to discriminate. Neither do the results conclusively disprove this hypothesis. Further tests will be necessary.

There is, however, some weak support for the idea that capital markets are improving over the period. Lance Davis would probably find this agreeable, in spite of his own conclusion that capital markets improved over this period in all areas of the country except the Pacific region.[6]

EARNINGS/ASSETS TESTS

Lance Davis' technique for estimating differences in interest rates from information given in the Comptroller of the Currency reports involves collecting gross earnings and the amount of assets that would be expected to earn interest. The ratio of gross earnings to earnings assets is the approximation of the interest rate on loans.[7] The Davis technique has been utilized frequently, although later writers, as previously noted, were critical of the exact technique used by Davis.

As the earnings/asset technique has been found acceptable enough to have its details a matter of discussion, it is interesting to compare the results of earnings/asset tests with the tests on interest rates paid on deposits. Most of the California state savings banks reported their gross earnings every year after 1880. Net earnings are reported for all banks in 1879 and for savings banks after 1880. As gross earnings divided by interest-earning assets are the most generally accepted interest rate proxy, we will use it for comparisons wherever possible.

It is necessary to participate in the controversy over the definition of earning assets. This study includes all loans, holdings of stocks, bonds and securities of all types, and funds due from banks and bankers. The state banks did not hold United States bonds primarily as backing for notes, therefore Smiley's reasons for their exclusion are not pertinent here. In addition, examination of individual bank's breakdown of the asset item "invested in stocks, bonds and warrants" reveals that the bulk of these assets were of private issue with some large portion of local government paper. In 1879, assets were reported in a manner which makes the separation of earnings assets impossible. Therefore 1879 shows the ratio of net earnings to total assets, while the other years reported show gross earnings and assets as defined above.

The rates developed for California state banks are lower than the Smiley and Davis rates for the Pacific region (see table 3). Specifically San Francisco, and San Francisco plus Los Angeles, is lower than their Pacific region reserve city bank figures every year.

TABLE 3

GROSS EARNINGS/EARNING ASSETS
COMPARISON
Urban/Reserve City
(percent)

	1889	1894	1899	1905
California State Banks (S.F. + L.A.)	6.87	6.91	5.13	3.39
Davis (Pacific Region)	7.80	7.22	6.18	5.07
Smiley (Pacific Region)	8.22	7.76	6.73	6.11

The rate for all rural banks is also lower with these calculations for California state banks than the rates calculated by Davis and Smiley for California national banks, as shown in table 4 (see table 35, in the appendix, for detailed analysis).

TABLE 4

GROSS EARNINGS/EARNING ASSETS COMPARISON
Non-Reserve City
(percent)

	1889	1894	1899	1905
California State Banks	8.28	8.24	6.58	4.46
Davis	8.81	8.12	7.91	7.06
Smiley	9.61	9.04	9.82	7.84

There are several possible explanations for the different results shown in tables 3 and 4. It could reflect a difference in profitability between state and national banks, or between savings banks and commercial banks. The second possibility seems unlikely in California, as savings banks could easily have become commercial banks and there were so few restrictions on the investment activities of either. It is also possible the difference between these results and those from other studies reflect the different definitions of earning assets or the difference between California and the remainder of the Pacific region.[8]

The percentages can be compared with interest rates paid on deposits by county. Gross earnings percentages should always exceed the interest paid on deposits to allow the bank to meet expenses for maintaining accounts. Comparison of table 35 with table 34 in the appendix reveals that this is true in all cases where gross earnings are used. As one might expect, where net earnings are divided by total assets, the mean ratio is very low and falls below interest paid to depositors in every comparison (see table 5). The spread between interest earned and interest paid ranges from 0.7 to 5.4 percent. The differences are highest in the southern counties and much lower in San Francisco than elsewhere. There does not seem to be a pronounced decline in the differences over time overall, but there is some decrease in the south. This data seems to indicate that San Francisco was quite competitive even in 1884 and the southern counties were being integrated into the market during the time period studied.

TABLE 5

COMPARISON OF INTEREST RECEIVED PROXY
WITH INTEREST PAID
(percent)

	S.F.	North	Central	South	Rural
1879					
Interest Received[a]	4.120	4.400	3.690	3.470	3.780
Interest Paid[b]	6.718	7.506	7.348	8.127	7.594
1884					
Interest Received	5.000	-	-	-	7.000
Interest Paid	3.871	4.562	4.508	-	4.466
1889					
Interest Received	5.700	-	7.860	11.330	8.280
Interest Paid	4.425	5.000	4.692	4.540	4.794
1894					
Interest Received	6.440	7.250	8.260	8.730	8.350
Interest Paid	4.621	4.642	4.788	4.133	4.615
1898					
Interest Received	5.110	6.980	6.970	5.220	6.670
Interest Paid	3.687	3.707	4.166	3.743	3.982
1905					
Interest Received	4.630	4.980	5.140	3.780	4.460
Interest Paid	3.393	3.221	3.453	3.578	3.481

[a] From table 35, appendix.
[b] From table, average of term and ordinary.

When pairwise comparisons were made between the different regions, earnings to asset ratios show few significant differences (see table 6). The differences do not occur frequently over time and occur more frequently in comparisons involving the south. San Francisco ratios differ significantly from other areas with great frequency. The difference between San Francisco and all other regions increases sharply in 1889, then declines slowly.

TABLE 6

DIFFERENCE IN MEAN
GROSS EARNINGS/EARNING ASSETS

Test	1879	1884	1889	1894	1898	1905
North vs Central	0	-	-	0	0	0
North vs South	0	-	-	0	*	0
Central vs South	0	-	*	0	*	*
S.F. vs North	0	-	-	0	0	0
S.F. vs Central	0	-	*	*	*	0
S.F. vs South	0	-	*	*	0	0
S.F. vs others	0	0	*	*	*	0

-       insufficient data
0   difference not significant
*   difference significant at ninety percent level of confidence

For details see table 36, appendix.

Differences occur in three of five comparisons of San Francisco and other central counties, in two of four comparisons with the south and in no comparisons with the north.

It is possible the decline in differences in earning/assets between San Francisco and the rest of the state occurs because, as Los Angeles develops a financial center the ratios there tend to decrease. To test this, San Francisco and Los Angeles were combined and compared with the rest of the state for years 1889 and 1905. The results are shown in table 7.

TABLE 7

GROSS EARNINGS/EARNING ASSETS
SAN FRANCISCO + LOS ANGELES VS. OTHER AREAS

	difference	t-value
1889	-1.41	-1.38
1894	-1.44	0.92
1899	-1.54	1.13
1905	-0.53	-1.10

This change lessens the difference between urban and rural areas. Los Angeles banks have ratios much greater than San Francisco banks, however, this difference is declining throughout the period. It does appear that differences between urban and rural areas are not declining, although the differences are statistically significant at the ninety percent level only in 1889.

The gross earnings tests show little variation between areas. The differences do not seem to subside over time. San Francisco banks show ratios that clearly differ from other areas. A great decline in this difference over time is not apparent.

Neither the differences in interest paid on deposits, nor the differences in earnings to asset ratios provide strong support for the hypothesized existence of rural monopolies. Neither do these differences show a definite tendency to decline over time. The hypothesized decline in travel and information costs may not have occurred, or if it did, it may not have caused detectable improvement in the financial markets. Further tests may add evidence to resolve the controversies.

NOTES

1. Richard Sylla, "Federal Policy, Banking Market Structure, and Capital Mobilization in the United States, 1863-1913," *Journal of Economic History* 19 (December 1969), pp. 657-686. Lance Davis, "The Investment Market, 1870-1914: The Evolution of a National Market," *Journal of Economic History* 25 (September 1965), pp. 355-399. Gene Smiley, "Interest Rate Movements in the United States, 1888-1913," *Journal of Economic History* 35 (September 1973), pp. 591-620. John James, "Banking Market Structure, Risk, and the Pattern of Local Interest Rates in the United States, 1893-1911," *Review of Economics and Statistics* 58 (November 1976), pp. 453-462.

2. Board of Bank Commissioners, State of California, *Report to the Legislature* (Sacramento: State of California, 1879).

3. According the Benjamin Wright, *Banking in California, 1849-1910* (San Francisco: H.S. Crocker Co., 1910), p. 114, almost all joint stock banks recognized two classes of deposit accounts: ordinary and term. Ordinary deposits were payable on demand and term deposits required six months notice before withdrawal. Term deposits, he reports, usually paid 0.2% higher interest. Wright also states, on page 39, that commercial banks also carried interest-bearing savings deposits, but ias the commissioner did not require them to report these deposits separately until 1909, the savings deposits are not segregated in the reports. John Jay Knox, *A History of Banking in the United States* (New York: Augustus M. Kelley, 1969; originally published 1903), reports on page 187 that it was customary for country banks everywhere to pay interest on all deposits and issue certificates of deposit bearing interest which was paid whenever the money was left for the stated period of time.

4. It should be noted that the chief method of acquiring funds for California banks was deposit creation, as they were barred from circulating notes (see Chapter II). J. Van Fenstermaker notes that deposit funds were early an important part of the money supply, hence a source of funds for banks. Even in the antebellum period he reports note issue was never more than twice deposit balances and in some

years deposits exceeded notes outstanding. J. Van Fenstermaker, "The Statistics of American Commercial Banking," *Journal of Economic History* 25 (1965), p. 409.

5. Sylla, passim.

6. Davis, p. 356.

7. *Ibid.*

8. Kerry A. Odell, *Capital Mobilization and Regional Financial Markets: The Pacific Coast States, 1850-1920*, (New York & London: Garland Publishing, Inc., 1992) explores this issue.

V

EVIDENCE ON MONOPOLY POWER

REAL ESTATE LENDING

California has had high real estate appreciation since the first pickax struck gold. While the cyclical nature of that appreciation is undeniable, it has rarely been more dramatic than the fluctuations of the financial markets or even of real capital. Then and now, real estate was considered an important investment for consumers and businesses alike. In such an atmosphere, banks could not afford to distain such an opportunity for lending.

Virtually all state banks and savings banks engaged in the real estate mortgage business. In most years before 1907, all commercial, savings, private banks, and banks in the process of liquidating, gave details of their mortgage loans by total amount loaned to each county in California or state outside California. A few listed each individual loan, and some merely named the counties and total amount loaned without providing individual amounts for each county. This information provides evidence on the ability or willingness of financial institutions to make loans to somewhat distant areas.

Savings banks committed the largest percentage of their assets to loans on real estate, but the larger resources of the commercial banks made them as important a loan source. Private banks seemed to serve this market less frequently. In all years most banks reporting no loans on real estate are foreign banks, branches of foreign banks, or private banks. In 1878, only three banks among the state commercial and savings banks did not loan on real estate (four percent of all banks, see table 37, appendix). The percentage rose slightly in 1884 to six percent (five banks). When private banks began reporting in 1889, the percentage of banks which did not loan on real estate rises to ten percent (seventeen banks, nine of which were private banks), but falls in 1894 to six percent. The percentage rises to twelve percent in 1899 and eighteen percent in 1905, indicating banks are beginning to specialize. This is supported by observations which indicate the increase in state banks with no loans on real estate is due to commercial banks withdrawing from this market in later years.

San Francisco bankers seem to have been particularly aggressive in real estate lending. There were several large banks that had very large sums invested in mortgages. German Savings and Loan, for example had over $9 million in real estate loans in 1878 (92% of their assets), Hibernia Savings had about $1.5 million (85% of their assets) and two other San Francisco savings banks had over $500,000 loaned in this category. The Bank of California was lending over $1 million (10% of their assets), which included loans on real estate in Arizona, Missouri, and Nevada.[1]

Much of their real estate lending occurred on property located outside San Francisco. Benjamin Wright reports that in 1880, San Francisco banks had 23 percent of all of their mortgage loans on property outside the city. Most of this lending was on grain-producing land, and Wright contends this was a profitable line of business.[2]

By 1892, the state had fifty-four counties and San Francisco banks were lending to forty-four counties. The ten counties receiving no mortgage funds from San Francisco savings banks are all small and in remote mountain areas. These banks loaned seventy six million dollars that year on real estate, with thirty six million outside the city. The counties receiving over one million dollars in loan funds from San Francisco banks were Alameda, Fresno, Los Angeles, Tulare, San Bernardino, San Luis Obispo, Santa Clara, and Stanislaus, but the total loaned to these counties constitutes less than one-third of the seventy million dollars. Four million of the loans were on Oregon property and over $3 were on Washington state property.[3] In 1897, mortgage loans of San Francisco banks totaled about $77 million. Forty-eight percent went to areas outside San Francisco.

The German Savings Bank seems to have been consistently the most important bank in the mortgage market throughout the period. They were lending $9,248,133 in eight counties by 1878 and in thirty-eight counties in 1908. They were the first bank to lend on real estate outside the state and other San Francisco banks followed their example.[4] Perusal of the collected material from the Bank Commissioners' *Reports* reveals loans to all neighboring states as well as a few loans to distant states.[5]

San Francisco's invasion of other counties seems to have increased through the decades of the eighties and nineties, then began to decline. Wright says, "the rapid multiplication of savings banks in the interior of the state, as well as in the states contiguous to California has made competition keen, and the business outside of San Francisco has therefore been less desirable, resulting in a material reduction in these outside loans."[6]

IMPLICATIONS OF REAL ESTATE LENDING

The Sylla model relies on the existence of a discriminating monopolist to support the existence of differences in interest rates between urban and rural areas. The rural banker loans at high rates in the country and at low rates in the city. His monopoly in the rural area prevents the money borrowed from him in the city from being reloaned in the country in competition with him. If San Francisco bankers were in fact lending large amounts in rural areas, the only difference in interest rates that is likely to exist between counties would be that which was due to difference in cost. Therefore, it is important to develop data to verify whether this lending occurred.

Perusal of the Bank Commissioners' *Reports* reveals that San Francisco banks were lending in rural areas. For example, San Francisco Savings Union was lending in thirty-seven different counties in California in 1889. German Savings was lending in forty-one of the state's counties in 1894, and in other states.

It is also apparent that bankers outside San Francisco are were lending to areas distant from their office. Sacramento Bank is lending in twenty-one counties on July 1, 1889. Most banks in fact seem to be lending on real estate located in a county other than where the bank's offices are located.

Table 8 provides information on banks which reported details of their loans on real estate. There is little support for the contention that banks were prevented by transaction or information cost from lending outside their immediate neighborhood. Counties generally encompassed a fairly large geographic area in California, and banks loaned on real estate outside their home county with great frequency.

TABLE 8

REAL ESTATE LENDING
BY NUMBER OF COUNTIES

Number of Banks Reporting Loans in
Number of Counties

YEAR	1	2	3	4-10	11-20	>20
1878	26	17	6	22	6	3
	(33%)					
1884	28	12	21	20	7	0
	(32%)					
1889	81	31	14	31	9	4
	(48%)					
1894	94	51	39	50	14	6
	(37%)					
1899	79	56	34	52	10	0
	(34%)					
1905	159	78	32	62	8	4
	(46%)					
1905	w/o southern counties					
	(40%)					

further detail is provided in table 37, appendix.

Even as early as 1878 sixty-seven percent of the banks were lending outside their home county and thirty percent were lending on real estate in at least five different counties. It is consistently true that most banks were lending outside the county where the main office was located.

The most interesting feature of the table is the consistency of lending outside the county. Except for 1889 and 1905, the percentage of banks lending only in the home county is almost constant. The lending to other counties should increase as communication and transportation developments facilitate loans on distant property. The increase in the last year of the study, however, is predictable. The number of banks in the large counties in the southern part of the state increased dramatically after 1900. If southern counties are excluded from the analysis, the percentage of remaining banks lending in only one county drops considerably.

The data rather conclusively dispels the image of the local banker limited to allocating his funds between the local farmers and the one big city bank. It does not, however, contain proof that the market improved over time.

REAL ESTATE LOAN SOURCES

Further examination of the data on real estate lending may provide other generalizations. The information could provide some indirect evidence for the hypothesis that banks had local monopoly power. The number of banks located in each county has often been used as a measure of monopoly power.

TABLE 9

REAL ESTATE LOANS
number of savings banks reporting loans in the county

County	1878[1]	1884	1889	1894	1899	1905[2]
1. San Francisco	18	22	18	29	30	42
2. Alameda	23	20	22	37	35	46
3. Santa Clara	11	13	21	29	32	33
4. San Mateo	8	10	12	15	18	26
5. Santa Cruz	10	8	14	18	16	14
6. Contra Costa	13	15	15	16	18	22
7. Solano	16	15	19	26	22	27
8. Napa	11	14	16	19	18	15
9. Sonoma	19	18	23	28	20	23
10. Marin	10	10	15	14	15	18
11. Yolo	6	9	11	12	18	15
12. Sacramento	6	6	9	7	11	11
13. Sutter	8	5	7	9	9	11
14. San Joaquin	8	10	15	16	16	18
15. Stanislaus	10	10	16	19	18	21
16. Merced	14	13	14	19	11	16
17. San Benito	6	3	5	17	17	16
18. Monterey	10	9	16	28	21	26
19. Lake	3	4	8	8	7	10
20. Colusa [3]	12	11	17	15	14	19
21. Glenn (est. 1891)	-	-	-	19	18	15
22. Mendocino	8	8	12	19	11	20
23. Butte	10	6	16	22	18	18
24. Yuba	8	4	6	12	10	12
25. Tehama	6	7	13	13	11	11
26. Humboldt	6	5	8	13	13	7
27. Del Norte	0	0	0	0	0	4
28. Siskiyou	1	3	7	6	8	8
29. Trinity	1	1	2	1	1	2
30. Shasta	0	2	7	11	9	7
31. Modoc	0	3	4	4	5	3
32. Lassen	0	3	4	6	5	4
33. Plumas	1	1	1	0	2	1
34. Sierra	1	0	0	1	0	0
35. Nevada	2	2	8	5	3	3
36. Placer	5	5	11	16	11	14
37. El Dorado	0	1	5	7	7	6

TABLE 9 (CONTINUED)

REAL ESTATE LOANS
number of savings banks reporting loans in the county

County	1878[1]	1884	1889	1894	1899	1905[2]
38. Amador	1	2	3	2	4	5
39. Alpine	0	0	0	0	0	0
40. Calaveras	1	1	4	6	4	5
41. Tuolumne	0	0	1	2	3	2
42. Mariposa	2	0	4	4	4	1
43. Madera (e 1893)	-	-	-	15	13	11
44. Fresno[4]	12	15	27	51	33	29
45. Kings (e 1893)	-	-	-	20	21	12
46. Tulare[5]	14	9	19	39	32	20
47. Mono	1	1	1	0	0	20
48. Inyo	1	1	0	0	0	2
49. Kern	6	2	7	24	21	15
50. San Luis Obispo	7	7	12	20	21	23
51. Santa Barbara	6	1	8	19	17	23
52. Ventura	3	7	5	10	12	14
53. Los Angeles [6]	13	8	28	33	37	63
54. San Bernardino[7]	2	5	15	27	29	26
55. Riverside (e 1893)	-	-	-	25	25	26
56. Orange (e 1893)	-	-	1	17	24	29
57. San Diego[8]	7	3	17	17	17	21

(1) does not include private banks
(2) does not include banks in liquidation
(3) part of Colusa County became Glenn County in 1891
(4) part of Fresno County became Madera County in 1893
(5) part of Tulare County became King County in 1893
(6) part of Los Angeles became Orange County in 1889
(7) part of San Bernardino County became part of Riverside County in 1893
(8) part of San Diego County became part of Riverside County in 1893

However, if banks outside the area were also loan sources, any such test would over-estimate monopoly power. From instance, California had many counties with only one bank (table 23, appendix), but it is much less common to find a county with only one lending source (see table 9 and 10).

TABLE 10

COUNTIES WITH ONLY ONE LENDING SOURCE

IN YEAR	1878	1884	1889	1894	1899	1905
NUMBER	8	7	4	2	1	3
PERCENT	15.4	13.5	7.5	3.5	1.8	5.3

Table 8 indicates that banks did not make an increasing number of loans outside their own counties and, by table 10, (except for 1905) the counties limited to one loan source were diminishing. There were two possible explanations. Those banks who were early participants in the mortgage market on distant property could have increased their loans to other counties. It is also possible that loans from banks located in the county were starting to substitute for loans from banks outside the county. A more detailed examination of lending sources seems appropriate.

To determine whether each county was losing loan sources, it is necessary to check for trends in the average perentage of lenders located outside the county For each county, the lending sources for real estate were divided according to whether the lending institution was located inside or outside the county in which the real estate was located. Then the percentage of banks located outside the county was calculated. Table 11 reveals fairly constant ratios after 1878.

TABLE 11

PERCENTAGE OF LENDERS LOCATED OUTSIDE THE COUNTY

YEAR	1878	1884	1889	1894	1899	1905
PERCENT	82.1	73.5	71.0	74.3	76.8	71.6

A more detailed analysis county by county (table 12) reveals several trends consistent with a competitively developing capital market. San Francisco, the undisputed financial center of the West, seems to be facing more competition from outside banks, as its percentage of loan sources from outside the county rises over the period. Many of the more remote counties like San Mateo, Sutter, Siskiyou, and San Bernadino develop later to rely less on outside sources.

It is also obvious from table 12 banks outside the county are an important loan source for real estate mortgages. Most of the counties received more than fifty percent of their real estate loans from banks outside the county. In 1878 and 1884, all the counties except San Francisco had more that fifty percent of the lenders located outside the county. In 1889, San Luis Obispo, Los Angeles, and the then very large county of San Bernardino, (which included what is now Riverside County), joined the list with more lenders located in the county than without. This is undoubtedly due to the very large size of the county, because San Bernardino loses this position when Riverside banks move into the Riverside County category in 1889. Santa Cruz, Sacramento, Humboldt and Nevada counties show a drop in the percentage of lenders located outside the county that stays below fifty percent in most years after 1894. In the first of these four cases, the statistics are indicative of developing financial centers, although the second two cases occur along with low lending levels and few loans.

TABLE 12

PERCENTAGE OF LOAN SOURCES LOCATED OUTSIDE COUNTY

Borrowing County	1878	1884	1889	1894	1899	1905
1. San Francisco	16.6	13.6	5.6	20.7	43.3	35.7
2. Alameda	91.3	90.0	77.4	62.2	57.1	60.9
3. Santa Clara	54.5	61.5	71.4	65.5	59.4	60.6
4. San Mateo	100	100	100	93.3	94.4	88.5
5. Santa Cruz	70.0	75.0	57.1	44.4	37.5	28.6
6. Contra Costa	92.3	93.3	93.3	87.5	88.9	81.8
7. Solano	75.0	80.0	80.0	80.8	77.3	74.1
8. Napa	81.8	85.7	75.0	73.7	77.8	66.7
9. Sonoma	61.1	50.0	60.9	57.1	45.0	51.5
10. Marin	90.0	100	93.3	92.9	80.0	88.9
11. Yolo	83.3	77.8	72.7	75.0	72.2	66.7
12. Sacramento	50.0	50.0	55.6	42.9	54.6	36.4
13. Sutter	100	100	71.4	88.9	88.9	90.9
14. San Joaquin	62.5	60.0	66.7	68.8	68.8	66.7
15. Stanislaus	80.0	90.0	81.3	89.5	88.9	76.2
16. Merced	85.7	92.3	85.7	89.5	81.8	87.5
17. San Benito	83.3	66.7	80.0	76.5	82.4	75.0
18. Monterey	90.0	88.9	100	86.1	90.5	73.1
19. Lake	80 .0	50.0	100	75.0	71.4	80.0
20. Colusa	91.6	90.9	52.9	86.7	85.7	84.2
21. Glenn	-	-	-	89.5	88.9	86.7
22. Mendocino	62.5	75.0	66.7	73.7	90.9	75.0
23. Butte	80.0	66.7	75.0	77.3	72.2	83.3
24. Yuba	75.0	75.0	50.0	66.7	70.0	66.7
25. Tehama	83.3	85.7	84.6	84.6	81.8	90.9
26. Humboldt	83.3	60.0	62.5	46.2	46.2	28.6
27. Del Norte	-	-	-	-	-	75.0
28. Siskiyou	100	66.7	71.4	66.7	87.5	37.5

TABLE 12 (CONTINUED)

PERCENTAGE OF LOAN SOURCES LOCATED OUTSIDE COUNTY

Borrowing County	1878	1884	1889	1894	1899	1905
29. Trinity	100	100	100	100	100	50.0
30. Shasta	-	50.0	57.2	81.8	77.8	71.4
31. Modoc	-	100	50.0	75.0	100	66.7
32. Lassen	-	100	75.0	100	100	100
33. Plumas	100	100	100	-	100	100
34. Sierra	-	-	100	-	-	-
35. Nevada	50.0	50.0	62.5	20.0	66.7	40.0
36. Placer	100	100	63.6	62.5	90.9	78.6
37. El Dorado	-	100	80.0	85.7	85.7	66.7
38. Amador	100	100	100	100	75.0	80 .0
39. Alpine	-	-	-	-	-	-
40. Calaveras	100	100	100	100	100	80.0
41. Tuolumne	-	-	100	100	33.3	50.0
42. Mariposa	100	-	100	100	75.0	100
43. Madera	-	-	-	86.7	84.6	90.9
44. Fresno	91.6	86.7	85.2	84.3	93.9	72.4
45. Kings	-	-	-	85.0	81.0	75 .0
46. Tulare	100	88.9	78.9	84.6	72.4	80.0
47. Mono	-	100	100	-	87.0	100
48. Inyo	100	100	-	-	-	50.0
49. Kern	83.3	50.0	85.7	87.5	81.0	86.7
50. San Luis Obispo	85.7	85.7	33.3	70.0	76.2	69.6
51. Santa Barbara	83.3	100	87.5	79.0	76.5	87.0
52. Ventura	66.6	85.7	60.0	70.0	75.0	71.4
53. Los Angeles	76.9	75.0	39.3	48.5	51.4	33.3
54. San Bernardino	100	80.0	40.0	70.4	81.5	84.6
55. Riverside	-	-	-	72.0	76.0	84.6
56. Orange	-	-	0	82.4	79.2	79.3
57. San Diego	71.4	100	63.4	58.8	70.6	76.2

We do see the southern counties developing their own financial sources in later years. The percentage of lenders located outside those counties declined generally, and Los Angeles county particularly demonstrated this trend. The southern counties also demonstrate the sharp drop in outside lenders apparent for 1889 and 1905. It is probable that the rapid growth of this area in the last decade of the century caused a surge in demand met by forming new banks at the site rather than by looking to established banks in other areas.

There are other changes in the financial structure made apparent by table 12. San Francisco, the acknowledged financial center of the Pacific region, always has a substantially lower percentage of lenders located outside the county. In later years, however, there is increasing competition from financial institutions located outside the county. The percentage of loan sources located outside San Francisco rises over the twenty-seven year period from less than seventeen to more than thirty-five percent.

Although the percentage of lending located outside the county is very high for almost all counties, the largest loans were generally from banks located within the borrowing county. The percentage of funds coming from banks located outside the county is uniformly lower than the percentage of lenders located outside the county (see table 13).

TABLE 13

PERCENTAGE OF LOAN FUNDS FROM BANKS OUTSIDE THE COUNTY

County	1878	1884	1889	1894	1899	1905
1. San Francisco	0.1	0.1	*	0.2	0.7	1.7
2. Alameda	62.8	60.0	96.4	40.6	65.5	74.6
3. Santa Clara	21.8	22.3	60.4	47.8	46.1	9.2
4. San Mateo	100	100	100	85.7	77.3	86.1
5. Santa Cruz	37.6	31.7	7.1	8.8	5.0	3.1
6. Contra Costa	88.8	84.4	80.2	79.7	87.2	57.8
7. Solano	4.0	33.1	50.4	59.5	57.6	40.8
8. Napa	24.4	71.4	62.5	65.5	56.0	25.2
9. Sonoma	30.2	14.0	29.6	36.7	41.1	16.5
10. Marin	90.4	100	89.4	90.3	75.9	79.5
11. Yolo	64.5	12.3	18.4	26.2	69.6	21.1
12. Sacramento	5.0	12.9	33.8	31.6	32.7	18.3
13. Sutter	100	100	79.1	87.0	83.7	42.3
14. San Joaquin	15.3	15.0	31.3	31.6	11.9	13.3
15. Stanislaus	87.6	80.0	92.8	83.1	83.0	58.8
16. Merced	77.2	85.2	72.2	65.3	66.7	42.3
17. San Benito	64.3	40.8	49.7	55.4	41.8	36.6
18. Monterey	77.6	50.0	100	75.6	76.1	60.2
19. Lake	18.1	55.2	100	20.6	58.5	15.4
20. Colusa	79.9	69.2	66.1	65.3	71.9	62.3
21. Glenn	-	-	-	80.0	50.3	61.6
22. Mendocino	21.7	67.1	8.5	11.7	74.5	41.3
23. Butte	85.4	48.9	42.2	40.2	51.8	76.9
24. Yuba	43.4	51.8	-	47.4	60.8	44.7
25. Tehama	64.4	54.2	9.2	73.5	66.6	96.0
26. Humboldt	34.4	43.9	18.9	29.5	20.8	0.7
27. Del Norte	-	-	-	-	-	48.8
28. Siskiyou	100	5.7	5.6	6.3	82.1	20.6
29. Trinity	100	100	100	100	100	10.9
30. Shasta	-	19.7	19.7	77.9	56.5	18.8

TABLE 13 (CONTINUED)

PERCENTAGE OF LOAN FUNDS FROM BANKS
OUTSIDE THE COUNTY

County	1878	1884	1889	1894	1899	1905
31. Modoc	-	100	50.6	97.5	100	85.3
32. Lassen	-	100	9.6	100	100	100
33. Plumas	100	0	100	-	100	100
34. Sierra	-	-	-	100	-	-
35. Nevada	83.5	27.5	35.1	21.4	100	2.6
36. Placer	100	100	80.9	19.7	97.1	93.7
37. El Dorado	-	100	91.2	84.4	40.3	15.6
38. Amador	100	100	100	100	100	5.9
39. Alpine	-	-	-	-	-	-
40. Calaveras	100	100	100	100	100	19.0
41. Tuoluome	-	-	100	100	66.7	2.8
42. Mariposa	100	-	100	100	86.2	100
43. Madera	-	-	-	95.0	95.3	93.5
44. Fresno	96.0	84.0	92.8	50.1	94.7	79.1
45. Kings	-	-	-	94.5	72.4	46.7
46. Tulare	100	42.7	89.0	87.8	87.0	89.0
47. Mono	-	0	0	-	-	100
48. Inyo	100	100	-	-	-	10.6
49. Kern	71.9	28.2	83.3	80.4	67.9	95.3
50. San Luis Obispo	61.9	86.9	6.5	59.5	55.4	67.1
51. Santa Barbara	96.4	100	98.5	84.4	74.2	94.0
52. Ventura	67.1	78.5	56.4	56.7	54.5	73.0
53. Los Angeles	42.0	48.5	64.2	43.2	12.4	26.4
54. San Bernardino	100	93.2	15.6	64.6	89.2	69.0
55. Riverside	-	-	-	66.8	69.2	94.0
56. Orange	-	-	-	46.4	82.3	84.2
57. San Diego	69.3	100	68.4	44.7	27.7	16.5

-   no loans   *insignificant amount

While the small size of many of the counties made the opening or closing of one bank a significant event in many of the years shown, examination of the consistantly growing counties close to San Francisco; Alameda, Santa Clara,San Mateo, Santa Cruz, Marin, seems to be consistent with the growth of local banks in response to increasing loan demand. As another check, the average percentage of total real estate lending which came from outside the county shown on table 14 highlights the increased self-sufficiency of counties by 1905.

TABLE 14

AVERAGE PERCENTAGE OF FUNDS FROM OUTSIDE THE COUNTY

YEAR	1878	1884	1889	1894	1899	1905
PERCENT	68.1	59.9	57.6	61.9	66.2	49.9

The number of counties receiving more than fifty percent of their real estate loan funds from sources located outside the county is shown in table 15. The developing financial independence noted for 1905 is again apparent. The exclusion of the southern counties causes the ratio to drop even further, to 37.2%. When southern counties separated from other areas, it can be observed that they still receive most of their funds from other areas. Although Los Angeles is, by 1905, receiving only 26.4%, San Diego only 16.5%, and Kings and Inyo counties are receiving less than fifty percent of their very small amount of mortgage funds from outside the county, all other counties were still mostly dependent on outside sources. Seventy-one percent of the southern counties received more than half their total loans from other counties, and the average amount of funds these counties borrowed from outside banks was 67.5 percent. Although San Francisco is receiving a minute portion of its funds from outside the county, it should be noted that the figures indicate a steady rise in this proportion.[7]

TABLE 15

COUNTIES RECEIVING MORE THAN HALF
THEIR FUNDS FROM OUTSIDE THE COUNTY

YEAR	1878	1884	1889	1894	1899	1905
PERCENT	69.8	67.4	61.7	63.5	78.8	49.1

The pattern revealed by this data is decreasing dependence on central sources of funds, although the percentage of funds and lenders located outside the county falls from 1878 to sometime before 1894 and rises briefly for 1894 and 1899 before the sharp drop in 1905. Southern California follows this pattern with some lag.

While mortgage loans may not accurately reflect the markets for other types of loans they certainly should not be related. Wright feelt that real estate and commercial borrowers were in close competition for funds from bankers. His information on mortgage interest rates indicated that the rates of interest on commercial loans mortgages were very similar.[8]

In this presentation of data, there is no support for Sylla's local monopoly hypothesis. The market for real estate loans in California reveals too pronounced a tendency to lend over wide geographic areas. Local monopolies may have existed, but they certainly did not characterize the market.

EFFECT OF DISTANCE ON LENDING

The question still remains of whether distance was a deterrent to prospective lenders. It is possible intracounty lending occurred mostly between contingent or neighboring counties. The following test was designed to provide evidence on this point.

The largest sources of loans were several large San Francisco savings banks. A test was developed to determine the general effect of distance on amounts loaned. The relationship between a particular bank, or set of banks, lending to a particular county and the distance to the county was estimated along with other variables expected to affect the relationship. The basic hypothesis tested is that bankers in rural areas were able to charge higher interest rates when lending on real estate, as large distances (with attendant high information and transaction costs) made it uneconomical for banks outside the area to compete with local banks. The test was a least squares regression to determine the value of coefficients for

$$\frac{L_i^j}{P^j} = a_0 + a_1 d_i^j + a_2 N^j$$

where

i	$= 1,2...n$ where i is a specific bank
j	$= 1,2...n$ where j represents the county where the real estate is located
L_i^j	is the dollar amount of loans of bank i to county j
P^j	is the population of county j
d_i^j	is the distance from bank i to the center of population center of county j
N^j	is the number of banks located in county j.[9]

If distance was a barrier the amount loaned per capita by any or all banks tested should decrease, the greater the distance between the real estate and the lending sources. The coefficient a_1 should be significant and negative. A larger number of banks in a county should discourage loans from outside the county causing a negative coefficient. It is also possible that the number of banks in a county would increase if the county were further from potential competition from a financial center.

The results using both one active lender and then five lenders located in San Francisco in 1889 were similar (see table 16).[10] The coefficient a_1 is not significant. Distance has not been proved a factor discouraging these banks from lending on real estate. The coefficient a_2 is surprisingly positive, although not significant. A positive sign could result from a high demand for funds in any county causing increased local bank formation as well as increased loans from outside sources. It is also reassuring to note there is no correlation between the number of banks in a county and that county's distance from San Francisco's relatively abundant capital.

TABLE 16

REGRESSION RESULTS

$a_0 = 3.7815$

$a_1 = 0.0072$ $(z = -0.0138)$

$a_2 = 0.2239$ $(z = 0.0165)$

The results of this test indicate that in 1889, distance did not create barriers of high risk or information cost which would allow local monopolies to exist.

CONCENTRATION AND SERVICE

Although the difficulties of developing an index of concentration have been discussed, it seems wise to compute traditional measures of concentration using our data.

Applying the usual test for concentration involves taking a few of the largest banks and determining their percentage of total assets, deposits, or capital. As many counties in the years mentioned actually had only one bank, it is possible to measure only the percentage of the market controlled by the one largest bank. Table 17 shows the results using assets as a market-share measure in 1889.

TABLE 17

PERCENTAGE OF TOTAL ASSETS HELD BY THE ONE LARGEST BANK, 1889[11]

Category	Number of Counties	% in category
Less than 25%	3	5
29-50	12	22
59-75	11	20
75-100	4	7
100	13	24
no banks	12	22

By contemporary standards, this appears to be a concentrated market. But while modern standards are imprecise, historical standards are almost non-existent. It does appear that cities are less concentrated than rural areas, but both the number of banks and the demand for banking services are greater.

Rondo Cameron has developed a test for the service or coverage an area received from the banking community. The Cameron index has been used previously by Richard Keehn.[12] It is the number of bank offices in a market multiplied by ten thousand and divided by the population of the area. If the index is greater than one, service is termed adequate. The results of the test for 1889 shows that of the counties with banks, only seven have "inadequate" service. These seven counties are San Francisco, Alameda, Contra Costa, Marin, Sacramento, Colusa and Santa Barbara. In 1889, these were well developed areas and, except for Santa Barbara, were adjacent to San Francisco county. It is very possible that the large San Francisco banks were able to service the customers in these areas without the benefit of extra offices. No significant differences in the index are revealed when the average Cameron indexes for different regions is compared.[13]

It is concluded that these tests of concentration are not highly useful. These results were expected from previous attempts to use these tests in other situations. Indeed, Irving Schwerger and John McGee found, when testing various measures of concentration, that differences in interest rates in small towns corresponds more closely to differences in the number of banks in an area than to other frequently used measures of concentration.[14]

BARRIERS TO ENTRY

Richard Sylla attributed the inhibition of banking to the high capital requirement for national banks and the tax on bank notes for state banks. It was also noted that the number of national banks located in California increased rapidly after 1900, the year capital requirements for national banks in rural areas were lowered. To determine whether high capital requirements were a barrier to national bank formation in California, the capital paid in coin was examined for commercial and savings banks in 1879, 1889, and 1899 and for private banks in 1899.

Table 18 reveals that most of the existing state banks would have been able to meet the national banking system's capital requirements. Eighty percent of all savings and commercial banks could meet the $50,000 in paid-up capital required in 1879. In later years, the amount of paid-up capital seems to fall. This is verified by the data presented in table 19, which shows the average amount of paid-up capital declines generally for all categories.

TABLE 18

AMOUNT OF CAPITAL PAID IN COIN
COMMERCIAL, SAVINGS AND PRIVATE BANKS
1879, 1889, 1899

All Banks*	Percentage of Banks in each Category		
	1879	1889	1899
Less than $25,000	8.20	11.80	16.80
$25,000 - $50,000	6.80	23.70	29.50
over $50,000	85.00	64.50	55.70
Commercial Banks	**1879**	**1889**	**1899**
Less than $25,000	9.00	9.70	10.20
$25,000 - $50,000	7.30	27.50	31.30
over $50,000	83.70	62.80	58.50
Savings Banks	**1879**	**1889**	**1899**
Less than $25,000	5.60	22.70	30.70
$25,000 - $50,000	5.60	4.60	25.00
over $50,000	88.80	72.70	44.30

Private Banks

		1899
Less than $25,000		43.80
$25,000 - $50,000	(no reports)	25.00
over $50,000		31.20

* 1879 and 1889 include only savings and commercial banks

TABLE 19

AVERAGE AMOUNT OF PAID-UP CAPITAL
($ THOUSAND)

	1879	1884	1889	1894	1899
All banks					145.7
Commercial banks	427.3	346.3	333.8	-	156.0
Savings banks	195.1	204.9	195.6	149.7	144.4
Private banks	-	-	112.5	-	47.3

CORRESPONDENT DEPOSITS

The Sylla model predicts that rural bankers would deposit funds in city banks to receive the interest they paid in preference to making local loans. His model does not allow for city banks depositing funds in rural banks, however, city bankers certainly kept deposits at other banks also. City banks used "correspondent" banks in the eastern United States and in foreign countries to facilitate transfers of funds and other commercial transactions. If differences between urban and rural banks in the percentage of bank funds deposited with other banks show up in examination of banks' balance statements, it could add support to the Sylla model.[15]

The amount of money due from banks and bankers was converted to a percentage of each bank's total assets. These percentages were then averaged for commercial banks in rural areas and for banks in the major cities. The balance statements for January 1 are used to avoid normal seasonal fluctuation.

TABLE 20

AMOUNT DUE FROM BANKS AND BANKERS AS A PERCENTAGE OF TOTAL ASSETS

	1889	1899
Urban banks *	7.57%	13.40
Rural banks	7.45	14.00

* defined as San Francisco in 1889 and San Francisco plus Los Angeles in 1899

The average ratios in urban and rural areas are nearly identical. Using the t-value test for difference in means of proportions, the computed t-value is 0.0784 for 1889 and -0.2090 for 1899. This test indicated that there was no significant difference in the means at a ninety-nine level of confidence. Country banks did not have a higher percentage of funds due from other banks. There is some possibility that the country bankers' deposits in the city banks are offset in the average ratios by city bankers depositing funds in other city banks, but it is an indication which does not support the Sylla model.

Further research, however, indicates that the seasonality factor may be important. Given agricultural cycles, country banks would be "loaned up" in January. When the test was repeated for July, country banks more frequently had significantly higher proportions of assets due from bankers.

PROFIT

If rural banks possessed some monopoly power while urban banks operated under the pressure of competition, it would be expected that rural banks would experience a higher level of profits. Although there are a variety of methods of measuring profits, all of the methods are likely to result in some inaccuracy in the results. The ratio of net earnings to total assets is one technique. It is difficult to make comparisons on this basis because of the small amount of data available

Some variation in profit might be revealed by variation in the return paid out to owners of the banks. Many savings banks reported the dividends paid, and the ratio of such dividends to paid-in capital. The results of comparing these rates are reported in table 21. The most important comparison is between San Francisco and other counties. There is a significant difference in the dividend rate of return on capital only for 1879. The difference is apparent for 1879 when San Francisco is compared with each part of the state, and differences between San Francisco and the South show up in 1899 and 1905 as well. Differences between areas are not revealed in either of the two years selected for testing.

TABLE 21

VARIATION IN RATE OF DIVIDENDS ON PAID-UP CAPITAL

Comparison	1879	1884	1889	1894	1899	1905
All other counties vs S.F.	*	0	0	0	0	0
S.F. vs Rural N	*	0	0	0	0	0
S.F. vs Rural C	*	0	0	0	0	0
S.F. vs Rural S	*	-	0	0	*	*
Rural N vs Rural C	0	-	-	0	-	-
Rural N vs Rural S	0	-	-	0	-	-
Rural S vs Rural C	0	-	-	0	-	-

-	not tested
0	no significant difference
*	difference significant at the ninety percent level of confidence

NOTES

1. Bank Commissioners *Reports*, June 30, 1878.

2. Benjamin Wright, *Banking in California, 1849-1940* (San Francisco: H.S. Croker Co., 1910), pp. 114-117.

3. *Ibid.*, pp. 114-116.

4. *Ibid.*, p. 115.

5. Bank Commissioners, *Reports*. Illinois frequently received loans from San Francisco banks.

6. Wright, p. 115.

7. This observation contrasts with a statement by Wright, p. 116. "The interior savings banks have never cared to take revenge on San Francisco for entering their fields." It could be that the trend toward increased loans from outside the county reversed itself between 1905 and 1908, or that commercial banks were the source of San Francisco's loans from outside the county.

8. Wright, p. 161.

9. The population for each county is from the US Department of Commerce, Bureau of the Census, United States *Census of Population 1890*. (Washington, D.C. 1890). Distance from San Francisco to each county was straight line distance estimated from California State Board of Railroad Commissioners, Official Railway Map of California (San Francisco, 1903).

10. The one bank test used German Savings and Loan. The four lenders added were Hibernia Savings and Loan, San Francisco Savings Union, Savings and Loan Society of San Francisco, and Security Savings Bank for the five bank test.

11. Computed from the balance statements for July 1, 1889 in the Board of Bank Commissioners, *Report to the Legislature*, appendix fold-out summary of statements.

12. Richard Keehn "Federal Bank Policy, Bank Market Structure and Bank Performance: Wisconsin, 1863-1914," *Business History Review* 48 (Spring 1974), p. 7.

13. Comparisons are made with the average of the Cameron index for the northern, central and southern regions. There were no differences significant at the ninety-nine percent level. 1899 is also tested. Seven counties yield index numbers under one. These counties are San Francisco, Alameda, San Mateo, and Marin, in the Bay area. Other counties with a low Cameron index are Mendocino, Tehema and Fresno. Again, it is observed that these counties, with the exception of Mendocino and Tehema, are not the remote areas where poor bank service is expected.

14. Irving Schwerger and John McGee "Chicago Banking," *Journal of Business* 234 (July 1961), pp. 201-366. Quoted in Paul Meyer, "Price Discrimination, Regional Loan Rates, and the Structure of the Banking Industry," *Journal of Finance* 22 (March 1967), p. 37. Lionel Kalish and R.A. Gilbert, "The Influence of Bank Regulation on the Operating Efficiency of Commercial Banks," *Journal of Finance* 28 (December 1976), p. 1292, is an example of some other techniques which use some measure of population per banking office.

15. Richard Sylla, "Federal Policy, Banking, Market Structure and Capital Mobilization in the United States, 1863-1913," *Journal of Economic History* 19 (December 1969), p. 684, does a similar analysis of the amount due from banks, the results of which support his model.

VI

SUMMARY AND CONCLUSIONS

FINANCIAL HISTORY

The study of financial history is necessary to provide data for testing the relationship between money and credit and the level of output in the economy. Understanding this relationship may help predict or prevent business cycles. It could also make it possible to increase the rate of development and growth of an economy. Most traditional theories of how countries can achieve efficient capital markets have developed from the study of the financial history of the United States. Yet knowledge of the development of the American economy is seriously incomplete, and will remain so as long as there is the lack of a satisfactory explanation for the behavior of an industry as vital as banking. Relatively little work has been completed in this area and much of the research completed in the last three decades altered previously held views about the structure of the financial institutions, and their behavior.

The early nineteenth century has received more of the attention of economic historians than the latter part of the century. Yet this later period corresponds with the most rapid industrialization in the United States. The 1965 work of Lance Davis stands as the most important early study of this period. The methods he used to detect differences in interest rates in different parts of the country establish the standard technique for later researchers. His findings indicate that there were imperfections in the capital market in the late nineteenth century and that capital mobility increased between 1870 and 1914.

Richard Sylla also has written a widely accepted article on the period. He theorizes that the federal government and provisions of the National Banking System served to restrain the growth of the financial industry. Specifically, Sylla feels the tax on bank notes and the requirements for paid-up capital created a two-tiered banking system. Banking in the cities was competitive, but rural bankers have a monopoly in their local market. This created a system which drained capital from rural areas to the urban areas.

Generally, economic theory predicts that if local monopolies exist in rural areas and a competitive market exists in urban areas, relative lending will be lower in rural areas and interest rates will be higher. Also, monopolies may exist temporarily because of a lack of demand in the market, or the information or transportation costs create barriers to entry. They are not likely to persist unless reinforced by other, probably legal, restrictions on entry. It should also be noted that a monopolist banker who can practice perfect discrimination will not restrict output, although he will charge a higher average interest rate.

DATA ON STATE BANKS

Almost all of the recent studies of nineteenth-century United States banking have depended on data from the reports of the Comptroller of the Currency. These reports do not include information on state banks. However, during most of the nineteenth century most of the banks in the country were chartered by the state, rather than the federal government. Therefore, the majority of the banks were not considered when the standard studies of the banking structure were completed.

This occurred because data on the state banks is less accessible to researchers. The state banks reported with much less consistency than national banks and each state used a different reporting system. The accessibility of state bank data can improve only by study on a state-by-state basis. The only work other of this type done to date is represented by the efforts of Richard Keehn, who attempted to locate and incorporate information on state banks in his studies of Wisconsin banking.

The addition of statistics on state banks to the base of data on national banks could substantially improve the accuracy of studies of bank structure and behavior. It could also be useful for studies on regional economic development. The development of a region has a great deal in common with overall development of an economy.

The current study sought to alleviate this problem by collecting statistics on banking in California for the years 1878 to 1905 from the Reports of the California Board of Bank Commissioners. A study of the causal relationship between financial intermediaries' behavior or structure and economic growth was not the purpose of this study, but it is expected that the results could be of some assistance to those attempting such studies. Results of this analysis can also be used to suggest whether the studies using only national banking data produced accurate results.

CALIFORNIA'S FREE BANKING ENVIRONMENT

California had few legal inhibitions on banking activity. Economic theory would suggest the lack of these restrictions would lead to a competitive atmosphere. The tests completed here were attempts to determine the extent of the barriers to capital mobility created by information and transportation costs.

What direct information was available on interest rates has been gathered. This included the interest rates charges on loans by thirty-nine banks in 1879, only one of which was located in San Francisco. These interest rates decline with increased distance from San Francisco. Dividing the state into geographic regions revealed consistency between banks in each area.

Because information on interest charges on loans was not available for other years, other attempts were made to discern differences in interest rates between regions. There is more information on the interest rates that were paid by banks to their depositors. This information was used to test for differences between cities and rural areas and between different parts of the state. The results reveal no consistent differences, and the scattered differences do not decrease in frequency over time.

Differences were more frequently significant when a proxy for interest rates was used. The proxy, developed by Lance Davis and modified very slightly in this study, is the ratio of gross or net earnings to earnings assets. This proxy for interest rates revealed differences which seem to disappear rather suddenly by 1905. Both the Davis proxy and the interest paid on deposits revealed significant differences most frequently in comparisons involving the southern rural areas. There is some indication that the southern part of the state may have been isolated and experiencing higher interest rates. This difference does not appear to decline over the time period covered.

REAL ESTATE LENDING

A study of the pattern of real estate lending also used some of the detailed information available in the bank commissioners' reports. Each bank reported the total amount of loans on real estate in each county in the state. Collection and processing of this information allowed the reconstruction of lending and capital flows. The data revealed several trends in the market. Almost all banks participated in real estate lending. Most banks loaned on real estate which was located at some distance from the bank office, and almost every county relied on loan sources located far from the property which served as security for the loan. These trends appear in every one of the six years studied.

The real estate loan information shows that San Francisco banks made loans throughout the state and serviced almost all of the demand for real estate loans in the city. Other towns also seem to follow this pattern in their banks' lending, but their customers also frequently went outside the county to seek loan funds.

The real estate lending also seems to indicate some isolation of the southern counties. As the economy there grew and prospered, the necessary extra capital appears to have been generated by local bank formation rather than by relying on existing banks as sources of capital.

The study of intracounty real estate loans also reveals the danger of using traditional measures of bank concentration which assume the loan sources are limited to banks within the local area. Very few counties were dependent entirely on local banks for loans.

EFFECT OF DISTANCE ON LENDING

The movement of capital does not seem, from this information, to have been greatly inhibited by distance. This was further verified by a regression analysis of San Francisco banks' lending. The regression reveals that distances from San Francisco to the collateral property was not a significant factor in the amount of funds loaned on the property.

The sketch of the late nineteenth-century California capital market which emerges from the data that have been collected is of competitive behavior of banking firms. Capital generally seems to have moved into an area in response to increased demand signaled by higher interest rates.

PRICE DISCRIMINATION

If the Sylla model is accurate for the California market, the rural banker had the ability to divide his customers into separate markets and charge each rural borrower the highest interest rate they would pay. In other words, he had the ability to price discriminate in the local market. The average interest rate charged in the less competitive rural market should have been greater than the average interest rate observed in the competitive urban market. The pattern of interest rates observed in California does not provide strong support for the Sylla model. Some tests revealed higher interest rates in rural area, but they were not significantly higher in most cases.

Sylla felt that the tendency of rural bankers to deposit funds in city banks in preference to making local loans mobilized capital and caused it to move from rural areas to the cities, and that this movement aided development. It is also true that his assumed local monopolist could not price discriminate if he was forced to compete with city bankers' lending in the rural areas. All indications of the study of real estate lending counter Sylla's conclusions. It is apparent that, in the California real estate market the capital flowed freely from the urban areas to the rural areas and between rural areas.

CAPITAL FLOWS

Other tests completed also tend to counter the Sylla model. It does not appear that California banks were kept from joining the national banking system by high capital requirements. Most of the state banks would have been able to meet the capital requirements of the national banking system. Sylla also predicts that, since the mechanism for the flow of capital to the cities was the rural bankers' deposits in city banks, rural bankers would have held a larger percentage of their assets in the form of bank deposits than would city banks. Although all banks, city and rural, could have money due from other banks for reasons which have nothing to do with monopoly power, significantly higher numbers for country banks indicates support for the Sylla hypothesis. From the available information, it does not appear that California rural bankers had more deposits in other banks than city bankers. For January, the balance statement item for funds due from other banks as a percentage of total assets is almost identical for urban and rural banks. Different results for summer months indicate a need for more study of this relationship.

EVOLUTION OF THE CAPITAL MARKET

Lance Davis' study indicates an improved capital market in later years of this period. An improvement in the capital market would be indicated by declining differences in interest rates throughout the state, and by increased capital flows to areas where interest rates are higher. This study of California does not indicate a trend of this type. There is some hint of a decline in interest rates when the Davis interest proxy is used, but these trends are not revealed in the interest paid to depositors. The real estate study does not indicate increased mobility of capital. Capital seems to have been moving throughout the state with comparative ease in all years studied.

This study makes several contributions to economic history. Although the tests do not disprove the Sylla model, they do raise some strong doubt about its validity for California. Some evidence had been presented which reflects on the Davis portrayal of the capital market, also making its relevance for California doubtful. The contribution of newly available data on interest rates and real estate lending should greatly assist others reconstructing the history of California banking. Regional development is, after all, a special case of economic development and new information on the rapid transition California made in the late nineteenth century could be useful to those who are looking for the necessary conditions for development of an economy.

APPENDIX

TABLE 22

CONTENT OF REPORTS TO BANK COMMISSIONERS

I. Commercial Banks and Savings Banks: Balance Statement

Assets

Bank lot and buildings
Real estate taken by foreclosure
Loan on real estate
Invested in bonds, stocks, warrants
Loans on other securities
Loans on personal securities
Money on hand
Deposits in other banks
Office furniture
Interest accrued
Other assets

Liabilities

Capital stock
Due depositors
Due banks and bankers
Dividends unpaid
Surplus

II. Names of directors, number of shares held by each, number of shares of capital stock issued and par value.

III. Invested in stocks and bonds by: class, amount loaned, value of securities.

IV. Loaned on other securities by: class, amount loaned, value of securities.

V. Deposits in other banks by: name of bank, amount.

VI. Loaned on real estate by: county, amount, total market value of property securing mortgages.

VII. Savings Banks (and Commercial Banks 1879)
Statistical Information
(In some years, most banks did not supply this information)

Total deposits
Number of deposit accounts open
Number of accounts opened during the past year
Number of accounts closed during the past year
Amount deposited during the past year
Amount withdrawn during the past year
Amount of dividends or interest paid to depositors
Rate per annum of such dividends or interest (term or ordinary)
Amount of dividends to stockholders during the past year
Rate per annum of dividends on paid up capital
Amount added to reserve fund during the past year
Amount of gross earnings during the past year
Amount of net earnings during the past year
Number of deposits less than $1,000
Number of deposits between $1,000 and $2,000
Number of deposits between $2,000 and $5,000
Number of deposits more than $5,000
Average amount in each deposit account

TABLE 23

NUMBER OF BANKS PER COUNTY

County	1878	1884	1889	1894	1899	1905
1. San Francisco	16	17	20	27	21	29
2. Alameda	2	2	6	14	12	19
3. Santa Clara	5	6	8	11	11	19
4. San Mateo	0	0	0	1	1	3
5. Santa Cruz	3	3	7	10	10	10
6. Contra Costa	1	1	1	2	2	4
7. Solano	4	5	5	6	4	9
8. Napa	2	2	4	5	3	5
9. Sonoma	7	9	10	12	10	17
10. Marin	1	0	1	2	1	2
11. Yolo	1	2	3	4	5	5
12. Sacramento	3	3	4	6	6	8
13. Sutter	0	0	1	1	1	1
14. San Joaquin	3	4	5	5	5	6
15. Stanislaus	2	1	3	4	3	5
16. Merced	2	2	2	3	3	2
17. San Benito	1	1	1	4	4	4
18. Monterey	1	1	0	5	4	7
19. Lake	2	2	0	3	2	2
20. Colusa	1	1	1	2	1	4
21. Glenn	0	1	2	2	2	3
22. Mendocino	3	3	4	5	2	5
23. Butte	2	2	4	5	5	8
24. Yuba	2	1	4	4	2	4
25. Tehama	1	1	1	2	1	3
26. Humboldt	1	1	3	7	6	6
27. Del Norte	0	0	0	0	0	1
28. Siskiyou	0	1	2	2	2	5
29. Trinity	0	0	0	0	0	1
30. Shasta	0	1	2	2	2	2
31. Modoc	0	0	1	1	0	1

TABLE 23 (CONTINUED)

NUMBER OF BANKS PER COUNTY

County	1878	1884	1889	1894	1899	1905
32. Lassen	0	0	0	1	0	0
33. Plumas	0	1	0	0	0	0
34. Sierra	1	0	0	0	0	0
35. Nevada	1	1	4	3	1	3
36. Placer	0	0	2	2	0	3
37. El Dorado	0	0	1	1	1	2
38. Amador	0	0	0	0	0	2
39. Alpine	0	0	0	0	0	0
40. Calaveras	0	0	0	1	0	1
41. Tuolumne	0	0	0	0	2	1
42. Mariposa	0	0	0	0	0	0
43. Madera	0	0	0	2	1	1
44. Fresno	1	2	4	8	2	8
45. Kings	0	0	2	2	4	3
46. Tulare	0	1	4	6	3	4
47. Mono	1	1	1	0	0	0
48. Inyo	0	0	0	0	0	2
49. Kern	1	1	1	4	3	3
50. San LuisObispo	1	1	4	8	5	8
51. Santa Barbara	1	0	1	4	5	8
52. Ventura	1	1	3	3	3	7
53. Los Angeles	3	3	19	24	21	51
54. San Bernadino	0	1	4	5	5	7
55. Riverside	0	0	5	10	10	6
56. Orange	2	2	4	7	8	9
57. San Diego	2	0	8	7	10	6
58. Imperial	0	0	0	0	0	2

TABLE 24

INTEREST CHARGED ON LOANS
1879

Reported by Commercial Banks
(Percent by month)

San Francisco
 Wells Fargo & Co.   1.00

Northern Counties
 Bank of Chico   1.25
 Citizen's County Bank-Nevada City   1.25
 Colusa County Bank-Colusa   1.25
 Farmer's Savings Bank-Lakeport   1.25
 Humboldt County Bank-Eureka   1.38
 Mendocino Discount Bank   1.25
 Bank of Napa   1.00
 Bank of Tehama-Red Bluff   1.25 & 1.5
 Bank of Woodland   1.00

Southern Counties
 Bank of Anaheim   1.50
 Commercial Bank of San Diego   1.38
 Commercial Bank of Los Angeles   1.25
 Farmers & Merchants Bank-Los Angeles   1.01
 Kern Valley Bank-Bakersfield   1.50
 Santa Barbara County Bank   1.01
 Bank of San Diego   1.50
 Bank of San Luis Obispo   1.50
 Bank of Ventura   1.50

TABLE 24 (CONTINUED)

INTEREST CHARGED ON LOANS
1879

Reported by Commercial Banks
(Percent by month)

Central Counties

Bank of Dixon	1.00
Farmers & Mechanics Bank-Heraldsburg	1.00
Bank of Fresno	1.25
Bank of Gilroy	1.25
Bank of Heraldsburg	1.01
Bank of Hollister	1.01&1.25, 1.5
Bank of Martinez	1.00
Petaluma Savings Bank	0.88
Sacramento Bank	0.88
Salinas City Bank	1.25
Bank of Santa Cruz County	1.19
Santa Rosa Bank	1.01
Bank of Santa Rosa	1.01
Sonoma Valley Bank	1.01
Bank of Suisun	1.01
Bank of Tomales	1.00
Bank of Vallejo	1.01
Bank of Visalia	1.50

TABLE 25

DIFFERENCES IN MEAN INTEREST RATE PAID ON DEPOSITS

RURAL NORTH VS. RURAL CENTRAL

	Ordinary	Term
1879		
Difference in mean	0.4105%	0.7280%
t or z value	t = -0.594	*z = 1.943
degrees of freedom	0.70	34
1884		
Difference in mean	0.4250%	
t or z value	t = 0.386	Insufficient
degrees of freedom	3	data
1889		
Difference in mean	0.4250%	
t or z value	t = 0.386	Insufficient
degrees of freedom	3	data
1894		
Difference in mean	0.3170%	0.0260%
t or z value	t = -1.222	t = 0.122
degrees of freedom	22	26
1899		
Difference in mean	-0.4320%	-0.4850%
t or z value	t = -1.399	t = -1.071
degrees of freedom	21	15
1905		
Difference in mean	-0.0720%	-0.3920%
t or z value	t = -0.453	t = -1.103
degrees of freedom	25	33

*	difference significant at ninety percent level of confidence
**	difference significant at ninety-five percent level of confidence
***	difference significant at ninety-nine percent level of confidence

TABLE 26

DIFFERENCES IN MEAN INTEREST RATE PAID ON DEPOSITS

RURAL NORTH VS. RURAL SOUTH

	Ordinary	Term
1879		
Difference in mean	-1.4580%	0.2160%
t or z value	*t = -2.299	t = 0.312
degrees of freedom	3	16
1884		
Difference in mean		
t or z value	Insufficient	Insufficient
data	data	data
degrees of freedom		
1889		
Difference in mean	1.2500%	
t or z value	t = 1.443	Insufficient
degrees of freedom	2	data
1894		
Difference in mean	0.8570%	0.1620%
t or z value	***t = 3.008	t = 0.673
degrees of freedom	19	20
1899		
Difference in mean	0.4950%	0.5670%
t or z value	***t = 3.989	**t = -2.627
degrees of freedom	14	13
1905		
Difference in mean	0.0080%	0.7210%
t or z value	**z = 0.037	**z = -2.062
degrees of freedom	36	36

    *   difference significant at ninety percent level of confidence
  **   difference significant at ninety-five percent level of confidence
***   difference significant at ninety-nine percent level of confidence

TABLE 27

DIFFERENCES IN MEAN INTEREST RATE PAID ON DEPOSITS

RURAL SOUTH VS. RURAL CENTRAL

	Ordinary	Term
1879		
Difference in mean	1.0470%	0.5120%
t or z value	t = 1.739	z = 1.428
degrees of freedom	8	32
1884		
Difference in mean		
t or z value	Insufficient	Insufficient
degrees of freedom	data	data
1889		
Difference in mean	-0.8250%	0.5230%
t or z value	t = -1.204	t = 1.166
degrees of freedom	5	11
1894		
Difference in mean	-1.1740%	-0.1360%
t or z value	***t = -5.822	z = 1.066
degrees of freedom	29	34
1899		
Difference in mean	-0.9270%	0.0820%
t or z value	***t = -4.481	t = 0.437
degrees of freedom	27	26
1905		
Difference in mean	-0.0800%	0.3290%
t or z value	z = -0.627	**z = 2.230
degrees of freedom	49	49

*   difference significant at ninety percent level of confidence
**   difference significant at ninety-five percent level of confidence
*** difference significant at ninety-nine percent level of confidence

TABLE 28

DIFFERENCES IN MEAN INTEREST RATE PAID ON DEPOSITS

ALL OTHER COUNTIES VS. SAN FRANCISCO

	Ordinary	Term
1879		
Difference in mean	0.5360%	0.7540%
t or z value	*t = -2.057	**z = -2.464
degrees of freedom	16	51
1884		
Difference in mean	-0.3110%	-0.1650%
t or z value	***t = -3.801	t = -.0993
degrees of freedom	9	10
1889		
Difference in mean	-0.0850%	-0.1410%
t or z value	t = -1.545	t = -0.807
degrees of freedom	15	15
1894		
Difference in mean	-0.1800%	-0.0230%
t or z value	z = 0.914	z = -0.182
degrees of freedom	46	50
1899		
Difference in mean	-0.1510%	-0.3220%
t or z value	z = -0.865	**z = -2.88
degrees of freedom	41	36
1905		
Difference in mean	0.0620%	-0.3380%
t or z value	z = 0.537	z = -0.968
degrees of freedom	66	53

* difference significant at ninety percent level of confidence
** difference significant at ninety-five percent level of confidence
*** difference significant at ninety-nine percent level of confidence

TABLE 29

DIFFERENCES IN MEAN INTEREST RATE PAID ON DEPOSITS

SAN FRANCISCO VS. RURAL NORTH

	Ordinary	Term
1879		
Difference in mean	-0.2000%	-1.3770%
t or z value	-0.848	**t = -2.642
degrees of freedom	6	17
1884		
Difference in mean	-0.6420%	-0.7400%
t or z value	*t = -2.295	***t = -4.636
degrees of freedom	7	4
1889		
Difference in mean	-0.8630%	Insufficient
t or z value	*t = -1.993	data
degrees of freedom	8	
1894		
Difference in mean	0.0540%	-0.0970%
t or z value	*t = 0.256	t = -0.392
degrees of freedom	15	14
1899		
Difference in mean	-0.1220%	0.0810%
t or z value	t= -0.908	t = 0.608
degrees of freedom	12	8
1905		
Difference in mean	0.0940%	0.2500%
t or z value	t = 0.770	t = 0.822
degrees of freedom	15	2

*   difference significant at ninety percent level of confidence
**   difference significant at ninety-five percent level of confidence
***   difference significant at ninety-nine percent level of confidence

TABLE 30

DIFFERENCES IN MEAN INTEREST RATE PAID ON DEPOSITS

SAN FRANCISCO VS. SOUTH

	Ordinary	Term
1879		
Difference in mean	-0.6580%	-1.1610%
t or z value	***t = -5.271	**t = -2.585
degrees of freedom	7	15
1884		
Difference in mean		
t or z value	Insufficient	Insufficient
degrees of freedom	data	data
1889		
Difference in mean	0.3870%	-0.6190%
t or z value	t = 1.165	t = -2.818
degrees of freedom	10	8
1894		
Difference in mean	0.9110%	0.0650%
t or z value	**t = 4.874	t = 0.485
degrees of freedom	22	22
1899		
Difference in mean	0.3730%	-0.4860%
t or z value	***t = 5.493	***t = -4.274
degrees of freedom	18	19
1905		
Difference in mean	0.1020%	-0.4170%
t or z value	z = 0.652	z = -1.362
degrees of freedom	39	36

   *   difference significant at ninety percent level of confidence
  **   difference significant at ninety-five percent level of confidence
 *** difference significant at ninety-nine percent level of confidence

TABLE 31

DIFFERENCES IN MEAN INTEREST RATE PAID ON DEPOSITS

SAN FRANCISCO VS. RURAL CENTRAL

	Ordinary	Term
1879		
Difference in mean	-0.6110%	-0.6490%
t or z value	t = -1.604	***t = -2.623
degrees of freedom	11	33
1884		
Difference in mean	-1.0670%	-0.2070%
t or z value	***t = -3.620	t = -0.703
degrees of freedom	7	9
1889		
Difference in mean	-0.4380%	-0.0960%
t or z value	t = -1.173	t = -0.351
degrees of freedom	11	15
1894		
Difference in mean	-0.2630%	-0.0710%
t or z value	t = -1.533	t = -0.577
degrees of freedom	25	28
1899		
Difference in mean	0.5540%	-0.4040%
t or z value	**t = -2.477	*t = -1.787
degrees of freedom	25	21
1905		
Difference in mean	-0.0220%	-0.1420%
t or z value	t = 0.114	t = -0.410
degrees of freedom	28	15

    *   difference significant at ninety percent level of confidence
   **   difference significant at ninety-five percent level of confidence
 *** difference significant at ninety-nine percent level of confidence

TABLE 32

DIFFERENCES IN MEAN INTEREST RATE PAID ON DEPOSITS

URBAN VS. RURAL
(SAN FRANCISCO, ALAMEDA, LOS ANGELES VS. ALL OTHERS)

	Ordinary	Term
1879		
Difference in mean	-0.6840%	-0.7430%
t or z value	*t = -1.759	**z = -2.358
degrees of freedom	16	51
1884		
Difference in mean	-0.7650%	-0.3160%
t or z value	**t = -2.569	t = -1.144
degrees of freedom	9	10
1889		
Difference in mean	-0.6350%	-0.1830%
t or z value	*t = -2.039	t = -0.708
degrees of freedom	15	18
1894		
Difference in mean	-0.3020%	-0.0660%
t or z value	z = -1.479	z = -0.564
degrees of freedom	46	50
1899		
Difference in mean	-0.1970%	-0.0240%
t or z value	z = -1.109	z = -0.157
degrees of freedom	41	36
1905		
Difference in mean	-0.0570%	0.2440%
t or z value	z = -0.582	*z = 1.840
degrees of freedom	66	53

*   difference significant at ninety percent level of confidence
**   difference significant at ninety-five percent level of confidence
***   difference significant at ninety-nine percent level of confidence

TABLE 33

DIFFERENCES IN MEAN INTEREST RATE PAID ON DEPOSITS

SAN FRANCISCO BAY AREA VS. OTHER COUNTIES

	Ordinary	Term
1879		
Difference in mean	-1.0780%	-1.0760%
t or z value	***t = -3.423	***z = -4.264
degrees of freedom	16	51
1884		
Difference in mean	-0.7650%	-0.4710%
t or z value	**t = -2.569	*t = -1.284
degrees of freedom	9	10
1889		
Difference in mean	-0.1930%	-0.4250%
t or z value	t = -0.569	*t = -1.759
degrees of freedom	15	18
1894		
Difference in mean	0.5330%	0.0380%
t or z value	***z = 2.634	z = 0.378
degrees of freedom	46	50
1899		
Difference in mean	0.2250%	-0.2980%
t or z value	z = 1.228	z = -1.948
degrees of freedom	41	36
1905		
Difference in mean	0.0190%	-0.3460%
t or z value	z = 0.173	*z = -1.734
degrees of freedom	66	53

* difference significant at ninety percent level of confidence
** difference significant at ninety-five percent level of confidence
*** difference significant at ninety-nine percent level of confidence

TABLE 34

INTEREST RATE PAID ON DEPOSITS

	North Ordinary	North Term	Central + S.F. Ordinary	Central + S.F. Term	South Ordinary	South Term
1879						
# banks reporting	2	10	7	26	3	8
Mean interest (%)	6.375	8.638	6.786	7.910	7.833	8.422
Standard deviation	0.375	1.462	0.839	0.708	0.623	1.242
1884						
# banks reporting	2	1	2	6	0	0
Mean interest (%)	4.125	5.000	4.550	4.467	-	-
Standard deviation	0.125	-	0.250	0.058	-	-
1889						
# banks reporting	1	0	4	10	3	3
Mean interest (%)	5.000	-	4.575	4.810	3.750	5.333
Standard deviation	-	-	0.851	0.666	0.612	0.471
1894						
# banks reporting	7	7	17	21	14	15
Mean interest (%)	4.157	5.129	4.474	5.103	3.300	4.967
Standard deviation	0.625	0.686	0.519	0.354	0.564	0.385
1898						
# banks reporting	5	2	18	15	11	13
Mean interest (%)	3.540	3.875	3.972	4.360	3.045	4.442
Standard deviation	0.320	0.125	0.637	0.599	0.143	0.280
1905						
# banks reporting	7	2	20	15	31	36
Mean interest (%)	3.143	3.300	3.215	3.692	3.135	4.021
Standard deviation	0.349	0.300	0.348	0.458	0.480	0.476

TABLE 34 (CONTINUED)

INTEREST RATE PAID ON DEPOSITS

	All Banks		S.F. Banks		Other Banks	
	Ordinary	**Term**	**Ordinary**	**Term**	**Ordinary**	**Term**
1879						
# banks reporting	18	52	6	9	12	45
Mean interest (%)	6.711	8.015	6.175	7.261	7.212	8.254
Standard deviation	0.828	1.044	0.191	0.228	1.176	1.207
1884						
# banks reporting	11	12	7	5	4	7
Mean interest (%)	3.794	4.425	3.483	4.260	4.337	4.543
Standard deviation	0.523	0.465	0.342	0.130	0.290	0.570
1889						
# banks reporting	17	20	9	7	8	13
Mean interest (%)	4.222	4.855	4.137	4.714	4.319	4.931
Standard deviation	0.691	0.552	0.387	0.143	0.845	0.664
1894						
# banks reporting	48	52	10	9	39	45
Mean interest (%)	4.031	5.055	4.211	5.032	4.009	5.060
Standard deviation	0.693	0.401	0.051	0.050	0.778	0.441
1898						
# banks reporting	43	38	9	8	34	30
Mean interest (%)	3.569	4.278	3.418	3.956	3.609	4.363
Standard deviation	0.578	0.465	0.142	0.157	0.640	0.483
1905						
# banks reporting	68	55	10	2	58	53
Mean interest (%)	3.175	3.888	3.237	3.550	3.164	3.901
Standard deviation	0.395	0.498	0.087	0.050	0.425	0.502

TABLE 34 (CONTINUED)

INTEREST RATE PAID ON DEPOSITS

	Rural Banks		S.F., Alameda, L.A.		Other Banks	
	Ordinary	Term	Ordinary	Term	Ordinary	Term
1879						
# banks reporting	11	39	7	14	9	24
Mean interest (%)	6.977	8.211	6.293	7.468	6.172	7.426
Standard deviation	0.932	1.114	0.033	0.516	0.207	0.516
1884						
# banks reporting	3	6	8	6	8	7
Mean interest (%)	4.350	4.583	3.585	4.267	3.585	4.229
Standard deviation	0.334	0.606	0.419	0.119	0.419	0.145
1889						
# banks reporting	6	9	11	11	10	11
Mean interest (%)	4.633	4.956	3.998	4.773	4.143	4.664
Standard deviation	0.715	0.793	0.484	0.157	0.368	0.240
1894						
# banks reporting	29	32	19	20	16	17
Mean interest (%)	4.150	5.080	3.848	5.014	4.386	5.086
Standard deviation	0.669	0.509	0.689	0.037	0.306	0.234
1898						
# banks reporting	20	17	23	21	16	14
Mean interest (%)	3.674	4.291	3.477	4.267	3.710	4.089
Standard deviation	0.492	0.395	0.629	0.515	0.633	0.544
1905						
# banks reporting	34	26	34	29	10	7
Mean interest (%)	3.203	3.759	3.146	4.003	3.188	3.586
Standard deviation	0.424	0.461	0.362	0.501	0.193	0.393

TABLE 35

MEAN RATIOS OF GROSS EARNINGS TO EARNING ASSETS

	San Franciso	North	Central	South	All Rural	San Francisco plus Los Angeles
1879						
(Net Earnings/Total Assets)						
Number of Banks Reporting	11	9	19	9	44	–
Mean (%)	4.12	4.40	3.69	3.46	3.78	–
Standard Deviation	1.85	2.43	1.27	2.44	1.78	–
1884						
Number of Banks Reporting	6	–	–	–	11	–
Mean (%)	5.00	–	–	–	7.00	–
Standard Deviation	0.078	–	–	–	0.02	–
1889						
Number of Banks Reporting	9	–	6	3	8	11
Mean (%)	5.70	–	7.86	11.33	8.28	6.87
Standard Deviation	1.24	–	0.91	1.49	1.07	2.77

TABLE 35 (CONTINUED)

MEAN RATIOS OF GROSS EARNINGS TO EARNING ASSETS

	San Franciso	North	Central	South	All Rural	San Francisco plus Los Angeles
1894						
Number of Banks Reporting	10	8	24	15	40	17
Mean (%)	6.44	7.25	8.26	8.73	8.35	6.91
Standard Deviation	1.04	1.68	1.57	3.85	2.50	2.15
1899						
Number of Banks Reporting	9	6	22	13	34	16
Mean (%)	5.11	6.98	6.97	5.22	6.67	5.13
Standard Deviation	1.15	2.91	1.70	0.95	2.53	1.14
1905						
Number of Banks Reporting	10	5	26	18	58	20
Mean (%)	4.63	4.98	5.14	3.78	4.46	3.93
Standard Deviation	1.44	0.79	1.72	1.90	1.91	1.77

TABLE 36

DIFFERENCE IN MEAN GROSS EARNINGS/EARNING ASSETS

	San Francisco vs. North	San Francisco vs. Central	San Francisco vs. South	San Francisco vs. All Others	North vs. South	Central vs. South	North vs. Central
1879							
(Net Earnings/Total Assets)							
Difference in Mean (%)	-0.32	0.43	0.65	0.34	0.93	0.22	0.71
t-Value	-0.28	0.76	0.68	0.56	0.78	1.37	1.01
degrees of freedom	17	28	18	53	15	26	25
1884							
Difference in Mean (%)	-	-	-	-0.02	-	-	-
t-Value	-	-	-	-2.105	-	-	-
degrees of freedom	-	-	-	15	-	-	-
1889							
Difference in Mean (%)	-	-2.1	-5.5	-2.04	-	-3.47	-
t-Value	-	*-3.62	*-6.66	*-3.36	-	*4.5	-
degrees of freedom	-	37	10	20	-	7	-

* significantly different at 90% level of confidence

- insufficient information for testing

TABLE 36 (CONTINUED)

DIFFERENCE IN MEAN GROSS EARNINGS/EARNING ASSETS

	San Francisco vs. North	San Francisco vs. Central	San Francisco vs. South	San Francisco vs. All Others	North vs. South	Central vs. South	North vs. Central
1894							
Difference in Mean (%)	-0.81	-1.82	-2.29	-1.80	-1.48	-0.47	-1.01
t-Value	-1.26	*-3.37	*-1.83	*-2.15	-1.02	-0.53	-1.55
degrees of freedom	16	34	23	55	21	37	30
1898							
Difference in Mean (%)	-1.87	-1.86	-0.11	-1.47	1.76	1.75	-0.01
t-Value	-1.77	*-3.01	-0.24	*-1.72	*2.01	*3.40	-0.01
degrees of freedom	13	29	20	47	17	33	26
1905							
Difference in Mean (%)	-0.35	-0.51	-0.85	0.17	1.20	1.36	-0.16
t-Value	-0.50	-0.83	1.23	0.20	1.36	*2.47	-0.20
degrees of freedom	13	34	26	66	21	42	29

* significantly different at 90% level of confidence   - insufficient information for testing

TABLE 37

NUMBER OF BANKS REPORTING LOANS IN

Year		1 county	2 counties	3 counties	4 counties	5-10 counties	11-20 counties	>20 counties	Total reports
1878	Savings	1	3	2	3	7	5	2	23
	Commercial	25	14	4	4	8	1	1	57
	Private	-	-	-	-	-	-	-	0
	Liquidating	-	-	-	-	-	-	-	0
	Total	26 (33%)	17	6	7	15	6	3	80
1884	Savings	1	0	2	2	7	5	0	17
	Commercial	27	12	19	2	9	2	7	1
	Private	-	-	-	-	-	0	-	0
	Liquidating	-	-	-	-	-	-	-	0
	Total	28 (32%)	12	21	4	16	7	0	88
1889	Savings	5	4	2	0	6	6	4	27
	Commercial	58	21	12	6	15	3	0	115
	Private	18	6	0	2	2	0	0	28
	Liquidating	-	-	-	-	-	-	-	0
	Total	81 (48%)	31	14	8	23	9	4	170

TABLE 37 (CONTINUED)

NUMBER OF BANKS REPORTING LOANS IN

		1 county	2 counties	3 counties	4 counties	5-10 counties	11-20 counties	>20 counties	Total reports
1894	Savings	10	10	6	5	15	8	5	59
	Commercial	64	35	26	14	15	5	1	160
	Private	9	3	2	1	0	0	0	15
	Liquidating	8	3	3	0	0	1	0	15
	Total	91 (37%)	51	37	20	30	14	6	249
1898	Savings	9	6	6	7	13	5	0	46
	Commercial	58	44	26	13	16	5	0	162
	Private	6	4	2	2	0	0	0	14
	Liquidating	6	2	0	1	0	0	0	9
	Total	79 (34%)	56	34	23	29	10	0	231
1905	Savings	31	19	12	10	20	6	4	102
	Commercial	117	57	19	11	21	2	0	227
	Private	11	2	1	0	0	0	0	14
	Total	159 (46%)	78	32	21	41	8	4	343

BIBLIOGRAPHY

Aigner, D. A. "On Estimation of an Econometric Model of Short Run Bank Behavior." *Journal of Econometrics* 1 (October 1973): 201-28.

Alhadoff, David A. *Monopoly and Competition in Banking.* Berkeley, California: University of California Press, 1954.

Anderson, Bernard Eric. "An Investigation into the Effects of Banking Structure on Aspects of Bank Behavior." Phd. dissertation, Ohio State University, 1964.

Andrew A. P. *Statistics for the United States, 1867-1909,* National Monetary Commission, S. Document 570. 61st Congress, 2nd session, 1910.

Armstrong, Leroy and Denny, J. O. *Financial California: An Historical Review of the Beginnings and Progress of Banking in the State.* San Francisco: The Coast Banker Publishing Co., 1916.

Baltensperger, Ernest. "Economics of Scale, Firm Size, and Concentration in Banking." *Journal of Money, Credit, and Banking* 4 (August 1972): 467-88.

_____. "The Precautionary Demand for Reserves." *American Economic Review* 64 (March 1974): 205-10.

Barnett, George E. *State Banks and Trust Companies Since the Passage of the National Bank Act,* National Monetary Commission, Vol. II. S. document no. 659. 61st Congress. 3rd session, 1911.

Barth, James R. and Bennett, James T. "Deposit Variability and Commercial Bank Cash Holdings." *Review of Economics and Statistics* 57 (May 1975): 238-41.

Baughman, James P. "Early American Checks: Forms and Functions." *Business History Review* 41 (Winter 1967): 421-35.

Bean, Walter. *California: An Interpretive History.* New York: San Francisco: McGraw-Hill, 1968.

Beckhart, Benjamin H., ed. *The New York Capital Market.* 4 vols. New York: Columbia University Press, 1931.

Benston, George J. "Economics of Scale and Financial Institutions." *Journal of Money, Credit and Banking* 4 (May 1972): 312-41.

_____. "The Optimum Banking Structure: Theory and Evidence." *Journal of Bank Research* 3 (Winter 1973): 220-37.

Berry, Thomas Sr. *Western Prices Before 1861.* Cambridge: Harvard University Press, 1943.

_____. *Early California: Gold, Prices, Trade.* Richmond: The Bostwick Press, 1984.

Blackford, Mansel G. "Banking and Bank Legislation in California, 1890-1915." *Business History Review* 47 (Winter 1973): 482-507.

Board of Bank Commissioners of the State of California. *Annual Reports to the Governor and the Legislature.* Sacramento: State Printing Office, 1878 to 1907.

Board of Governors of the Federal Reserve System. *Banking and Monetary Statistics.* Washington, D. C.: Board of Governors of the Federal Reserve System, 1943.

Bodfish, H. Morton, ed. *History of Building and Loan in the United States.* Chicago: US Building and Loan League, 1931.

Bourne, Edward G. *The History of the Surplus Revenue of 1837.* New York: Burt Franklin, 1865. Reprinted 1968.

Brealey, R. A. and Hodges, S. D. "Playing with Portfolios." *Journal of Finance* 30 (March 1975): 125-34.

Beckenridge, R. M. "Discount Rates in the Unites States." *Political Science Quarterly* 13 (1898): 129.

Brigham, Eugene F. and Pettit, R. Richardson. "Effects of Structure on Performance in the Savings and Loan Industry" in *Study of the Savings and Loan Industry* Vol. III. Irwin Friends, director. Federal Home Loan Bank Board, Washington, D. C.: U.S. Government Printing Office, 1969: 971-1211.

Brown, George F. Jr. and Lloyd, R. M. "Static Models of Bank Credit Expansion." *Journal of Financial and Quantitative Analysis* 6 (June 1971): 995-1014.

Building and Loan Association Commissioners, California. *Annual Report* 1893/94 to 1903/4.

Cagan, Philip. *Determinents and Effects of Changes in the Stock of Money 1875-1960.* New York: National Bureau of Economic Research, 1965.

_____. "The First 50 Years of the National Bank Act-Historical Appraisal." *Banking and Monetary Studies* ed. by Deane Carson. Homewood, IL: Richard D. Irwin, Inc., 1963.

California State Board of Equalization. *Biennial Reports* 1871/73 to 1877/79. Sacramento: CA State Board of Equalization.

California Board of Bank Commissioners. *Annual Reports*, 1880-1903/4.

California State Board of Railroad Commissioners. *Official Railway Map of California,* November 1903. San Francisco, 1903.

Cameron, Rondo, ed. *Banking and Economic Development: Some Lessons in History.* New York: Oxford University Press, 1972.

Cameron, Rondo. *Banking in the Early Stages of Industrialization: A Study in Comparative Economic History.* New York: Oxford University Press, 1967.

Chandler, L. V. "Monopolistic Elements in Commercial Banking." *Journal of Political Economy* 46 (February 1938): 1-22.

_____. *The Economics of Money and Banking* 6th ed. New York: Harper and Row, 1973.

Claude, Arthur Campbell. *The Development of Banking in Tennessee.* Nashville: Vanderbilt University Press, 1932.

Comptroller of the Currency, *Abstract of Reports of Condition of National Banks.* Various years. Washington, D.C.:GPO.

38th Congress 1st session. Senate Exec. doc. 50, 1864. *Report from the Commission of Internal Revenue, accompanied by an Abstract of the Banks, Associations, Corporations & Individuals doing a Banking Business.*

Cross, Ira B. *Financing an Empire: Banking in California.* 4 volumes. Chicago, San Francisco, Los Angeles: S. J. Clarke Publishing Co., 1927.

Crumb, J. "Banking Regulation in California." Phd. dissertation: University of California at Berkeley, 1935.

Culbertson, J. "The Term Structure of Interest Rates." *Quarterly Journal of Economics* 71 (November 1957): 485-517.

Darnell, J. C. "Does Banking Structure Spur Economic Growth?" *Federal Reserve Bank of Philadelphia Review* (November 1972): 14-22.

Davis, Andrew. *Origins of the National Banking System.* Washington National Monetary Commission, 1910.

Davis, Lance. "Capital Immobilities and Finance Capitalism: A Study of Economic Evolution in the United States, 1820-1920." *Explorations in Entrepreneurial History* 1 (Fall 1963): 88-105.

_____. "The Investments Market, 1870-1914: The Evolution of a National Market." *Journal of Economic History* 25 (September 1965): 355-99.

Davis, Lance and Legler, John. "The Government in the American Economy, 1815-1902: A Quantitative Study." *Journal of Economic History* 37 (December 1966): 532-33.

Davis, Lance and Douglass C. North. *Institutional Change and American Economic Growth*. Cambridge: Cambridge University Press, 1971.

Dewey, Davis R. *State Banking Before the Civil War*. Washington, D.C.: Government Printing Office, 1910.

Dillistin, William H. *Bank Note Reporters and Counterfeit Detectors 1826-66*. Numismatic Notes and Monographs. New York: American Numismatic Society, 1949.

Doti, James L. and Esmael Adibi. *Econometric Analysis with microTSP Student Software: An Applications Approach*. New Jersey: Prentice Hall, 1988.

Dreese, G. Richard. "Banks and Regional Economic Development." *Southern Economic Journal* 40 (April 1974): 647-56.

Dunke, Glenn S. *The Boom of the Eighties in Southern California*. San Marino, CA: Huntington Library, 1966. Originally printed 1944.

Easterlin, Richard A. "Interregional Differences in Per Capita Income, Population and Total Income, 1840-1950," in *Trends in the American Economy in the Nineteenth Century: Studies in Income and Wealth*. Vol. 24. Princeton: Princeton University Press for National Bureau of Economic Research, 1960.

Edwards, Franklin. "Concentration in Banking and its Effect on Business Loan Rates," *Review of Economics and Statistics* 46 (August 1964): 294-300.

Emery, John T. "Risk, Return and the Morphology of Commercial Banking." *Journal of Financial and Quantitative Analysis* 6 (March 1971): 763-81.

Engerman, Stanley. "A Note on the Economic Consequences of the Second Bank of the United States." *Journal of Political Economy* 78 (July/August 1970): 725-28.

Fankhauser, W. C. *A Financial History of California: Public Revenue, Debts and Expenditures.* Berkeley: University of California Press, 1913.

Federal Reserve Board. "Research on Banking Structure and Performance." *Bulletin* (April 1966 and November 1964).

Federal Reserve Committee on Branch, Group, and Chain Banking. "Branch Banking in California." Mimeographed 1932.

Ferris, John Alexander. *The Financial Economy of the United States, Illustrated and Some of the Causes which Retard the Progress of California.* New York: Augustus M. Kelley, 1969. Originally published 1867.

Fishlow, Albert. "Antebellum Interregional Trade Reconsidered." *American Economic Review: Papers and Proceedings* 54 (May 1964): 352-64.

Fraser, Donald R. and Ross, Peter S. "Bank Entry and Bank Performance." *Journal of Finance* 27 (March 1972): 65-78.

Fried, Joel. "Bank Portfolio Selection." *Journal of Financial and Quantitative Analysis* 5 (June 1970): 203-27.

Friedman, Milton and Schwartz, Anna Jacobson. *A Monetary History of the United States, 1867-1960*. Princeton: Princeton University Press, 1963.

Galbraith, John Kenneth. *Branch Banking and its Bearing on Agricultural Credit*. Lancaster, PA: University of Pennsylvania, 1934.

Gilbert, Gary G. and Longbrake, William A. "Part II, The Effects of Branching by Financial Institutions on Competition, Productive Efficiency, and Stability: An Examination of the Evidence." *Journal of Bank Research* 4 (Winter 1974): 298-307.

Glasner, David. *Free Banking and Monetary Reform*. New York: Cambridge University Press, 1989.

Goldfield, S. M. *Commercial Bank Behavior and Economic Activity*. Amsterdam: North Holland Publishing Co., 1966.

Goldsmith, Raymond. *Financial Intermediaries in the American Economy Since 1900*. New York: National Bureau of Economic Research, 1975.

_____. *Financial Structure and Development*. New Haven and London: Yale University Press, 1969.

_____. "The Quantitative International Comparison of Financial Structure and Development." *Journal of Economic History* 35 (March 1975): 216-37.

Goldy, Samuel N. *The Era of California's Supreme Industrial Possibilities*. San Jose, California: Press of Murson and Wright, 1903.

Gramley, Lyle E. *A Study of Scale Economies on Banking*. Kansas City, MO: Federal Reserve Bank of Kansas City, 1962.

Greef, A. O. *The Commercial Paper House in the United States*. Cambridge, MA: Harvard University Press, 1938.

Guttentag, Jack M. and Herman, Edward S. "Banking Structure and Performance." *The Bulletin of the Graduate School of Business Administration, Institute of Finance, New York University* (February 1967): 1-200.

Hammond, Bray. *Banks and Politics in America from the Revolution to the Civil War.* Princeton: Princeton University Press, 1957.

_____. "Free Banks and Corporations." *Journal of Political Economy* 44 (1936): 184-89.

_____. "Long and Short Term Credit in Early American Banking." *Quarterly Journal of Economics* 49 (November 1934): 79-103.

Hart, Oliver D. and Jaffee, Dwight M. "On the Application of Portfolio Theory to Depository Financial Intermediaries." *Review of Economic Studies* 41 (January 1974): 129-47.

Hasse, Adelaide R. *Index of Economic Materials in Documents of the United States: California, 1849-1904.* New York: Carnegie Institution of Washington, 1908.

Hildreth, Richard. *The History of Banks: To Which is Added a Demonstration of the Advantages and Necessity of Free Competition in the Business of Banking.* New York: Augustus M. Kelley, 1968. Originally published 1837.

Hinderliter, Roger and Rockoff, Hugh. "The Management of Reserves by Antebellum Banks in Eastern Financial Centers." *Explorations in Entrepreneurial History* 11 (Fall 1973): 37-54.

_____. "Banking Under the Gold Standard: An Analysis of Liquidity Management in the Leading Financial Centers." *Journal of Economics History* 36 (June 1976): 379-98.

Holmes, G. K. and Lord, J. S. "Report of Real Estate Mortgages in the United States," in Department of Congress, Bureau of Labor Statistics, 11th Census of the United States, vol. 12 (Washington 1895): 4-5.

Homan, I.S. *Banker's Almanac and Yearbook.* New York: International Publications Service, Annually since 1845.

Horwitz, Paul M. and Schull, Bernard. "The Impact of Branch Banking on Bank Performance." *The National Banking Review* 11 (December 1974): 143-89.

Jacobs, Donald. "The Interaction Effects of Restrictions on Branching and Other Bank Regulations." *Journal of Finance* 20 (May 1965): 332-49.

James, John A. "A Note on Interest Paid on New York Bankers' Balances in the Postbellum Period." *Business History Review* 50 (Summer 1976): 198-202.

_____. "Banking Market Structure, Risk, and the Pattern of Local Interest Rates in the United States 1893-1911." *Review of Economics and Statistics* 59 (November 1976): 453-62.

_____. "The Development of the National Money Market, 1893-1911." *Journal of Economic History* 36 (December 1976): 878-97.

Johnson, David A. *Founding the Far West: California, Oregon and Nevada, 1840-1890.* Berkeley: University of California Press, 1992.

Kalish, Lionel I. III, and Gilbert, R. Alton. "The Influence of Bank Regulation on the Operating Efficiency of Commercial Banks." *Journal of Finance* 28 (December 1973): 1287-1301.

Kane, E. J. and Malkiel, B. G. "Bank Portfolio Allocation, Deposit Variability and the Availability Doctrine." *Quarterly Journal of Economics* 79 (1965): 113-34.

Kaufman, G. "Bank Market Structure and Performance: The Evidence from Iowa." *Southern Economic Journal* 32 (April 1966): 429-39.

Keehn, Richard H. "Federal Bank Policy, Bank Market Structure and Bank Performance: Wisconsin, 1863-1914." *Business History Review* 48 (Spring 1974): 1-27.

_____. "Market Structure and Bank Performance: Wisconsin 1870-1900." Phd. dissertation, University of Wisconsin, 1972.

Keehn, Richard and Smiley, Gene. "Mortgage Lending by National Banks, 1890-1914." Paper presented at Western Economic Association Annual Meeting, San Francisco, June 1976.

Kessel, Rueben A. "The Cyclical Behavior of the Term Structure of Interest Rates." New York: National Bureau of Economic Research Occasional Paper 91, 1965.

Keyes, Emerson W. *A History of Savings Banks in the United States.* New York: B. Rhodes, 1878.

Kidner, Frank LeRoy. *California Business Cycles.* Berkeley and Los Angeles: University of California Press, 1946.

Klein, Michael A. "A Model of the Banking Firm." *Journal of Money, Credit, and Banking* 3 (May 1971): 205-18.

Knox, John Jay. *A History of Banking in the United States.* New York: Augustus M. Kelley, 1969. Originally published 1903.

Kohn, Ernest. *Branch Banking, Bank Mergers and the Public Interest.* New York: New York State Banking Department, January 1964.

Kohn, Ernest and Carlo, Carmen J. *The Competitive Impact of New Branches.* New York: New York State Banking Department, December 1969.

Korlinas, P. G. "A Model of Money, Credit and Economic Growth." *Kyklos* 27 (1974): 757-76.

Kross, Herman and Blyn, Martin. *A History of Financial Intermediaries.* New York: Random House, 1971.

Lanzellotti, R.F. and Saving, T.R. "State Branching Restrictions and the Availability of Branching Services: A Comment." *Journal of Money, Credit and Banking* 1 (November 1969): 778-88.

Lauch, Louis H. and Murphy, Neil B. "A Test of the Impact of Branching on Deposit Variability." *Journal of Financial and Quantitative Analysis* 5 (September 1970): 323-27.

Lee, E. S., Miller, A. R., Brainerd, C. P., and Easterlin, R. A. *Population Redistribution and Economic Growth in the United States,* 1870-1950. Philadelphia: American Philosophical Society, 1957.

Lister, Roger. *Bank Behavior, Regulation, and Economic Development: California, 1860-1910.* New York and London: Garland Publishing, Inc. 1993.

_____. "Market Structure and Economic Performance: California Banking 1890-1900." Paper presented at Western Economic Association June, 1977.

Longbrake, William A. "Productive Efficiency in Commercial Banking: The Impact of Legal Forms of Organization and Size." Manuscript published by Federal Deposit Insurance Corporation, 1943.

Lutz, Friedrich A. "The Structure of Interest Rates." *Quarterly Journal of Economics* 55 (November 1940): 36-63.

Macesich, George. "Sources of Monetary Disturbance in the United States 1834-1845." *Journal of Economic History* 20 (September 1960): 407-34.

Madeline, Sister M. Grace. *Monetary and Banking Theories of Jacksonian Democracy.* Philadelphia: Kennika, 1970. Originally published 1943.

Malkiel, Burton G. *The Term Structure of Interest Rates: Expectations and Behavior Patterns.* Princeton: Princeton University Press, 1966.

_____. *The Term Structure of Interest Rates: Theory and Empirical Evidence.* New York: McCaleb-Seiler, 1970.

Meiselman, David. *The Term Structure of Interest Rates.* Englewood Cliffs, N.J.: Prentice-Hall, 1962.

Meyer, Paul A. "Price Discrimination, Regional Loan Rates, and the Structure of the Banking Industry." *Journal of Finance* 22 (March 1967): 37-48.

Michaelson, Jacob B. *The Term Structure of Interest Rates: Financial Intermediaries and Debt Management.* New York and London: Intext Educational Publishers, 1973.

Minsky, Hyman P., ed. *California Banking in a Growing Economy 1946-1975.* Berkeley: University of California Printing Department, 1965.

Mints, Lloyd. *A History of Banking Theory.* Chicago: University of Chicago Press, 1945.

Morrison, George R. *Liquidity Preferences of Commercial Banks.* Chicago: University of Chicago Press, 1968.

Myers, Margaret G. *A Financial History of the United States.* New York and London: Columbia University Press, 1970.

_____. *The New York Money Market, Origins and Development.* New York: Columbia University Press, 1931.

Nash, Gerald D. *State Government and Economic Development: A History of Administrative Policies in California, 1849-1933.* Berkeley: Institute of Government Studies, University of California, 1964.

Odell, Kerry. *Capital Mobilization and Regional Financial Markets: The Pacific Coast States, 1850-1920.* New York and London: Garland Publishing, Inc., 1992.

Orr, Daniel and Mellon, W.G. "Stochastic Reserve Losses and Expansion of Bank Credit." *American Economic Review* 51 (September 1961): 614-23.

Pierson Doti, Lynne. "Banking in California: Some Evidence on Structure 1878-1905." Ph.D. dissertation. Riverside, CA: University of California, 1978.

_____. "Nationwide Branching: Some Lessons from California." *Essays in Business and Economic History* 9 (1991)

Pierson Doti, Lynne and Schweikart, Larry. *Banking in the American West: From the Gold Rush to Deregulation.* Norman, OK and London: University of Oklahoma Press, 1991.

_____. *California Bankers 1848-1993.* Needham Heights: Ginn Press, 1994.

Porter, Richard C. "A Model of Bank Portfolio Selection." *Yale Economic Essays 1* (Fall 1961): 323-59.

Posey, Rollin. "Profits of Commercial Banks." *Harvard Business Review* 8 (July 1930): 422-29.

Powell, John J. *The Golden State and its Resources.* San Francisco: Bacon and Company, 1874.

Pyle, David H. "On the Theory of Financial Intermediation." *Journal of Finance* 26 (June 1971): 737-48.

Redlich, Fritz. "American Banking and Growth in the Nineteenth Century: Epistemological Reflections." *Explorations in Entrepreneurial History* 14 (Spring 1973): 228-46.

_____. *The Molding of American Banking: Men and Ideas*. New York and London: Johnson Reprint Corp., 1968. Originally published 1947.

Riefler, W. W. *Money Rates and Money Markets in the United States*. New York: Harper and Brothers, 1930.

Robertson, Ross M. *The Comptroller and Bank Supervision*. Washington, D. C.: Office of the Comptroller of the Currency, 1968.

Rockoff, Hugh. "The Free Banking Era: A Reexamination." Ph.d. dissertation, University of Chicago, 1972.

_____. "The Free Banking Era: A Reexamination." *Journal of Money, Credit and Banking* 6 (May 1974): 154-72.

_____. "Money Prices and Banks in the Jacksonian Era," in the *Reinterpretation of American Economic History* ed. by Robert Fogel and Stanley Engerman. New York: Harper and Row, 1971: 448-58.

_____. "Regional Interest Rates and Bank Failures, 1870-1914," *Explorations in Economic History* 14 (January 1977): 90-95.

_____. "Varieties of Banking and Regional Economic Development in the United States, 1840-1860." *Journal of Economic History* 35 (March 1975): 160-181.

Salitore, Edward V. *California Information Almanac: Past, Present, Future*. Lakewood, CA: Edward V. Salitore, 1973.

Sanders, R. J. "Cross-Sectional Differences among Commercial Banks: Further Comment." *Journal of Financial Quantitative Analysis* 9 (December 1974): 1053-55.

Sechrest, Larry. *Free Banking: Theory, History, and a Laissez-Faire Model.* Westport, CN: Quorum Books, 1993.

Selgin, George A. *The Theory of Free Banking: Money Supply under Competitive Note Issue.* Totowa, NJ: Rowman and Littlefield, 1988.

Sharp, James Roger. *The Jacksonians vs. the Banks Politics in the States after the Panic of 1837.* New York: Columbia University Press, 1970.

Sharpe, William. "Capital Asset Prices: A Theory of Market Equilibrium Under Conditions of Risk." *Journal of Finance* 19 (September 1964): 425-42.

Sharpe, William F. *Portfolio Theory and Capital Markets.* New York: McGraw-Hill, 1970.

Smiley, Gene. "A Note on the Pre-1914 Development of the American Capital Market." Working Paper. Department of Economics. Marquette University, Milwaukee, Wisconsin (July 1977).

_____. "Interest Rate Movements in the United States 1888-1913." *Journal of Economic History* 35 (September 1975): 591-620.

_____. "Regional Differentials in Interest Rates in the United States, 1888-1913." Working Paper, Department of Economics, Marquette University, Milwaukee, Wisconsin (January 1976).

_____. "The Evolution and Structure of the National Banking System." Phd. dissertation, University of Iowa, 1973.

Smith, Walter B. *Economic Aspects of the 2nd Bank of the United States.* Cambridge, MA: Cambridge University Press, 1953.

Smith, Warren L. "Financial Intermediaries and Monetary Controls." *Quarterly Journal of Economics* 78 (November 1959): 533-53. Reprinted in Harold Wolf and Conrad Doenges, *Readings in Money and Banking*. New York: Appleton-Century-Crofts, 1968: 274-93.

Smith, William Paul. "Measures of Banking Structure and Competition." *Federal Reserve Bulletin* 51 (September 1965): 1212-22.

Stigler, George. "Imperfections in the Capital Market." *Journal of Political Economy* 75 (June 1967): 287-93.

_____. "Perfect Competition, Historically Contemplated." in *Essays in the History of Economics*. Chicago: University of Chicago Press: 234-67.

_____. "The Division of Labor is Limited by the Extent of the Market." *Journal of Political Economy* 59 (June 1951): 185-93.

Summer. William Graham. *A History of Banking in the United States*. New York: Augustus M. Kelley, 1971. Originally published 1896.

Sylla, Richard. "American Banking and Growth in the 19th Century" A Partial View of the Terrain." *Explorations in Entrepreneurial History* 9 (Winter 1971-1972): 40-55.

_____. "Federal Policy, Banking, Market Structure and Capital Mobilization in the United States, 1863-1913." *Journal of Economic History* 19 (December 1969): 657-86.

_____. "Financial Intermediaries in Economic History: Quantitative Research in the Seminal Hypothesis of Lance Davis and Alexander Gershenkron." In *Recent Developments in the Study of Business and Economic History: Essays in Memory of Herman E. Kross,* 230-36. Edited by R.E. Gallman. Greenwich, CN: Jai Press, 1977.

Taus, Esther Rogoff. *Central Banking Functions of the United States Treasury 1769-1941*. New York: Columbia University Press, 1943.

Temin, Peter. "The Economic Consequences of the Bank War." *Journal of Political Economy* 76 (1968): 257-74.

Temin, Peter. *The Jacksonian Economy*. USA: W. W. Norton, 1969.

Timberlake, Richard H. Jr. "The Specie Standard and Central Banking in the United States before 1860." *Journal of Economic History* 21 (September 1961): 318-41.

_____. "The Specie Circular and the Distribution of the Surplus." *Journal of Political Economy* 68 (April 1960): 109-17.

Trescott, Paul B. *Financing American Enterprise: The Story of Commercial Banking*. New York: Harper and Row, 1963.

U.S. Department of Commerce. Bureau of Census. *United States Census of Population: 1880, 1890, 1900*. Characteristics of the Population, California.

Van Fenstermaker, J. "The Statistics of American Commercial Banking, 1782-1818." *Journal of Economic History* 25 (1965): 400-10.

_____. *The Development of American Commercial Banking 1782-1837*. Ohio: Kent State University, 1965.

Vernon, Jack R. "Regulatory Barriers to Branching and Merger and Concentration on Banking Markets." *Southern Economic Journal* 37 (January 1971): 349-55.

Wacht, Richard F. "Branch Banking and Risk." *Journal of Financial and Quantitative Analysis* 3 (March 1968): 97-107.

White, Lawrence. *Free Banking in Britain: Theory, Experience, and Debate, 1800-1845.* New York: Cambridge University Press, 1984.

Williamson, Jeffrey G. and Swanson, Joseph A. "Explanations and Issues: A Prospectus for Quantitative Economic History." *Journal of Economic History* 1 (March 1971): 45-52.

Williamson, Jeffery. Late Nineteenth Century American Development: A General Equilibrium History. Cambridge: Cambridge University Press, 1974.

Wright, Benjamin Cooper. *Banking in California, 1849-1910.* San Francisco: H. S. Crocker Company, 1910.

INDEX